I0187117

Memoirs of a High School Dropout:

Secrets to Success

Samuel D. Hobbs

To my mom and dad, who have put up with me all of these years. Thank you for your continuing support.

Copyright © 2008 Samuel D. Hobbs

All rights reserved. No part of this book may be reproduced in any form or by any means without permission in writing from the publisher, Samuel D. Hobbs, sdhobbs@gmail.com.

Library of Congress Control Number: 2008900193

ISBN 978-0-6151-8643-6

PROLOGUE

WITH two months left to graduate, I dropped out of high school. And I can tell you, life has never been so great. I must warn you—if you decided to read this book hoping to find denunciation of high school dropouts, you will be disappointed. I am not here to condemn but to inform. I am not here to tell you how to pick yourself up once you fall but rather how to stay on your feet. This is the story of my life.

Just a note: I do not intend to say that I am right and you are wrong or try to push my personal beliefs on you. I am simply writing the way that I view the world. I do not wish for you to take offense, but instead to read with an open mind. These are a few of my thoughts and beliefs at the present. They may change in the future (and probably will), but I guess only time will tell.

In addition, some names have been changed for purposes of confidentiality.

ONE

'REBELLIOUS' may as well have been my middle name. I was never one to conform, never one to let others rule my life. I was an individual, and no one was going to take that from me. Consider an essay I wrote for an English class during my Junior year of high school. Although it is written in satire, I never informed my teacher of that. I let her assume the worst and worry about me like teachers so often do.

Surviving High School

His large, Greek nose wiggled as he played his harmonica in Mr. Rimouski's chemistry class. Thoughts of suicide filled his mind as he discovered a large, puss-filled pimple protruding from his upper lip. Let's face it: a teenager's life is hard. Life is filled with black heads, difficult classes, and the continual confrontation between parents and students related to grades, ditching classes, and friends of the opposite gender. How does anyone go from being a teen to an adult? How do they survive the ongoing suffering and endless torment inflicted by puberty and society's rules? In my high school, I have learned methods to make life trouble-free. I have learned secrets to success. Let me share these with you.

Cheating has a negative connotation with most adults, but there are many positive aspects commonly overlooked. For example, you can become popular by giving homework answers to jocks, cheerleaders, or others considered "cool." You can also get better grades by sharing answers with your peers, who use smaller, more informative words than most teachers use. High-tech methods also exist for sharing answers via cell phones, email, and instant messaging. It is even possible to use Google, an online search engine, on a cell phone during a test. The subject matter is easier to understand when summarized by services such as Sparknotes, one of many online learning resources. Using Sparknotes often results in better grades for students who do not have time to read the assigned books.

This brings up a question: is it unethical to cheat? I mean, is it "wrong" for a teacher or student to provide answers to homework and tests? I do not believe so. Recently in my history class, my regular teacher was in the hospital for an elective surgery. All of my classmates were ecstatic. History is one of those classes where the teacher insists that the students learn, making the fifty minutes of lecture almost unbearable. Mr. S., the substitute teacher assigned to our class, was perfect: an old man who was intent on having every student like him as a person.

Every day, our regular teacher called Mr. S. to inform him of quizzes, homework assignments, and even a unit exam to be completed in his absence. Seeking for our approval, Mr. S. allowed all of these assignments to be completed as "group work." Mr. S. even participated in many of the assignments by using the answer key provided by our teacher. These acts of kindness demonstrated by the surrogate teacher greatly benefited our grades and personal satisfaction while attending school. Full-time teachers can learn from the example set by Mr. S. Group participation increases individual morale and grades, thus increasing the school's academic ranking. Giving out answers also helps foster learning: it is much easier to know the objective of a question when you have the correct response ahead of time.

Now that you understand the benefits of cheating, you can focus your attention on eliminating undue stress by using relaxing drugs. One may think that these methods are "illegal" and/or "harmful." However, many drugs are illegal only because they are used in excess, leading to addiction. When used in moderation, these drugs are wonderful stress-relievers. For example, morphine, an illegal narcotic, is frequently prescribed in hospitals to calm anxious patients. Marijuana also has its benefits, helping ease chronic pain; preventing conditions such as glaucoma (the leading cause of blindness in the United States) and epileptic seizures; relieving nausea and vomiting, in turn promoting an adequate nutritional intake; and acting as an appetite stimulant. The former governor of New Mexico, as well as other political leaders, wanted to legalize marijuana because of its medicinal benefits. Although dependency and addiction may result from taking any drug, such issues can be dealt with later in life when things are less stressful.

Furthermore, stress can be eliminated by playing sports or pulling pranks. Sports such as football and wrestling shift aggression in a physically competitive way. It is satisfying to wrestle smaller, lightweight students who have not had the opportunity for proper training. This means that you can use prohibited holds and turn their humiliation into your enjoyment. Pranks can also be a great source of stress relief. Such pranks include sticking a "kick-me" sign on the back of another student's shirt or spreading an unkind rumor. One of my favorite pranks is toilet papering—the process of decorating another person's lawn, house, trees, or car by wrapping them in toilet paper (hence the name). These acts are done as deeds of friendship, fun, or dislike and exclusion. They refocus negative energy, turning it into a positive, friend-building experience. Pranks allow students to demonstrate leadership, initiation, cooperation, and creativity—all skills valuable for later in life.

Ditching class is another great way to relieve high school stress. There are two types of ditching: skipping a single class (usually to avoid a test) or skipping a full day. Skipping a single class is usually the easiest to accomplish. Many teachers do not take attendance, so it may seem as if you were never really absent. For other teachers, you may need to show up to be marked as present for class and leave early because you "feel sick" or have an orthodontist/doctor appointment. These are rather easy to fake since your teacher has probably never heard half of the diseases out there. I would suggest having strongyloidiasis or Creutzfeldt-Jakob Disease if you are struggling with a convincing condition.

If you have a persuasive voice, a single call to the administration office pretending to be your father or mother may be the simplest way out of class. This is especially easy because the administration never verifies whom it is that is calling, and an aide typically retrieves you with a signed pass. If you are questioned at all, you can glance at your wristwatch and state that your appointment is in fifteen minutes (giving an actual time is most convincing). Depending on your individual circumstances, you may need to reevaluate the situation and change your story.

In a recent anonymous poll, more than 80% of high school students admit to having ditched a class in the past year. That number does not include the many who may have ditched the day the poll was taken. School administrators seem to do little to stop this action because it requires too much effort on their part. The lack of reinforcing the "no ditching" rule has only made ditching more accepted by students and teachers alike. You should try it. More than 80% of high school students enjoy the benefits of skipping class while you sit at an uncomfortable desk, bored out of your mind.

If you are still having difficulty surviving high school, it may be nice to know that adults help students survive by encouraging the methods I have discussed. Oftentimes, teachers leave the classroom during a test or are distracted while grading other assignments, allowing students to cheat off each other's papers. High school employees hardly ever go out of their way to find out what sorts of "questionable" activities the students (or teachers) are involved in. In fact, many students smoke marijuana in the bathrooms everyday and are never caught. They also enjoy congregating across the street from the school, in clear view of the administration, to smoke a "joint" or get drunk. I'm sure that if a teacher did find marijuana on a student, he or she would have a relaxing evening with that student, possibly enjoying a hand of poker or "high-card."

In conclusion, high school does not have to be a boring and painful experience. All one has to do is keep a positive attitude and implement some or all of the stress-reducers I have suggested. Who cares that drugs can cause lung cancer, liver disease, heart disease, kidney failure, halitosis, and death? You will be popular by using them. And who cares if you end up with no education and no life? All that matters is how you feel right now. Besides, habits can always be broken when you are older and life isn't so stressful. So enjoy life during high school. No one is going to stop you.

TWO

TODAY I got this journal that my dad brought home from work. I had a pretty good day at school. In social studies, I watched a cool movie on the Incas and how they mummified children and sent them into the mountains. Math: same old, same old. Notes and homework. In Lang/lit, we started watching the movie <u>Fahrenheit 451</u>. It is really funny and cheesy. In PE, I wanted to play basketball, but Mr. Harry wouldn't let me since I missed the run ONCE, so I had to walk all period. In orchestra, I wasn't able to play my instrument because Ms. Silverton was gone. In that class, we did worksheets the whole period. Jacob and I were the first ones done with those. In science, we did a lab on rocks that I didn't finish.

When I got home, I did my homework. All I had for H.W. was math, so I finished with no problem. I then went outside and dribbled my basketball, but I didn't shoot because Jared's truck is always in the way. I dribbled until dad got home with Jared. Jared left in his truck to go to Evelyn's house and pick her up for a date or something. So, I got a few minutes of shooting hoops while Jared was gone.

When Jared got home, I ate dinner and dad gave me this journal, telling me that I should start writing in it. That is where I started writing. In a few minutes, me, dad, and Jess are planning to go on a jog like we did yesterday. I am going to take my basketball again and shoot some hoops. Hopefully, dad and Jess will want to play B. Ball with me. Well, I guess that is it for today.

Before I start, I think it is important to have a little bit of history of where my family is right now. Even though I hate sections of books that have a bunch of random information, I hope that this won't be too bad. As this book progresses forward, each person in my life will become clearer. But, for now, I think it is necessary for you to have a snapshot of life in the Hobbs' home.

I was born into a family with high standards and high hopes for the future. My father, Michael L. Hobbs, has a PhD in the field of Chemical Engineering, working at Sandia National Laboratories in Albuquerque, New Mexico doing top-secret research for the government. Although this may sound like a terrific job, it is really a desk job, working at the computer and making models. He probably isn't allowed to work "hands-on" because he almost burnt down one of the buildings at Brigham Young University while studying there. I find it ironic that while he helps in creating weapons of mass destruction, I have hopes of becoming a medical doctor and helping those who are hurt.

My mother, Celestine, has her Associates Degree in Business Administration. For the past few years, she has been working part time at my former high school's Seminary as a secretary. When I say part time, I mean about 6 hours per week. However, she has many things that she wants to accomplish in her life. She wants to further her education but has never found the time to take the necessary classes. She wants to lose weight (as all women do) yet always seems to put it off until tomorrow, or until the beginning of a new month, or until the New Year, or until convenient. Her newest dream is to work as a nanny, but she can't seem to find anyone who pays what she is really worth. It is always an adventure living with my mom.

I have three siblings, two of whom are married and one who is serving a mission for our church. My oldest brother, Jared, was married to Jennifer Francisco Sandoval in the Dominican Republic soon after serving his mission there. He is currently attending the University of New Mexico and majoring in Computer Science. He is a bona fide genius on the computer, so whenever I have questions, he's the one to call.

My sister, Jessica, is the next oldest. She was just married last year here in Albuquerque to Sebastian Dunlap. They are now living in Provo, Utah while attending BYU. My sister is majoring in English, though previously working on art education, and her husband is majoring in something like Public Relations and Communications. He is planning on going to Law School when he finishes his undergraduate studies.

Jacob is my last brother, though still older than I am. At a young age, he was an introvert. I was an all-out extrovert, though I was never too skilled at socializing. He and I never got along. Our personalities seemed to clash whenever we were around each other. Sharing a bedroom didn't help our antithetical personalities. This was one of the reasons we had to move out of our old house: to get that extra bedroom and separate me and Jacob. While I spent my time playing games and being with friends, Jacob spent hours in his room alone, reading whatever book interested him. Jacob is an interesting character. Though he enjoyed classic novels, he also enjoyed reading textbooks and memorizing poetry. In seventh grade, he started progressing at math like no one I've ever known. Every math competition he entered, he won. Everything he enjoyed, he excelled at. As it turns out, he was the first in my immediate family to drop out of high school. An aunt and a cousin dropped out years earlier.

Jacob grew smarter as time went on, but with genius comes an inherent problem. I have found that those with the "genius-gene" always tend to lack something else that is vitally important to a balanced life. You might think he lacked social skills, since geniuses are often stereotyped as "weird," but the truth is that as time went on, Jacob actually became an extrovert and enjoyed spending time with friends (also ironic—as he became more extroverted, I became more introverted, so even though we got along better, we still didn't click). The inherent problem with Jacob is that he has very little common sense.

When Jacob dropped out of high school his sophomore year, it was to go to college early. Jacob thought it was a great idea to accompany our sister to BYU so she wouldn't be alone. However, with this newfound freedom, Jacob blew his scholarship to BYU by taking classes that simply did not make any sense. He took math classes that he didn't have the prerequisites for. He took dance classes, including history of dance (in which he got a D). He took religion classes galore, including teachings of Isaiah. He took Hebrew. He took Egyptian. I still don't get what he was thinking, but that is characteristically Jacob. I love that kid.

This book is about me, the youngest child in my family. You could say that I followed my brother's example when I dropped out of high school, but that would in no way be accurate. He was too young; he did not have enough experience in the world. I am also young, a mere seventeen, but I have the experience and am ready to take on the challenges of the world. Again, I apologize for this section of the book, which may seem dull or unimportant to my theme. But, it was my family who helped me become the individual I am today. As you read, you will probably find a bit of each member of my family in me.

Before I go on, I think it is also important to know where I'm coming from. I was raised in the Church of Jesus Christ of Latter Day Saints, also known as the "Mormon" church. I do not intend to make this a religious publication, nor do I claim that anything written here has been passed as doctrine of my church. However, my beliefs have been an integral part of my growth, so they may inadvertently show in what I write. For the record: I don't have horns, and I don't have more than one mother. I only have three siblings, not thirteen (although I know a family with thirteen; I also know a family with twelve, each still living at home at age eighteen and younger). Sorry to disappoint anyone out there.

THREE

WHEN I was five years old, I was an active child. I spent a day in gymnastics but would not listen to anyone. All I did was run around and jump on the trampoline. Needless to say, my gymnastics experience was short lived.

Still in my 5th year, I started martial arts, hoping to become one of the ninjas that I saw so often on TV. Believing that one day I would make it to that level, I did not quit. I progressed to my green belt level (just before brown belt) and enjoyed fighting. However, my downfall was imminent due to one small foible of my character—laziness.

"ITES!" I shouted as my fist moved quickly through the air. I felt a drop of sweat roll from my forehead and drip off my jaw. My small gi fit tightly around my protruding abdomen and was riding up on my waist. I was big for my age, 130 pounds at the age of eleven. My mom, with the most endearing affection, called me her little chunky monkey. My peers at school ridiculed me, more on my mannerisms than on my weight. Yet at that age, I really didn't see the difference. I wasn't accepted, and I never fit in.

TV was a favorite pastime. I spent hours sitting on my parent's queen-sized bed, fixed on the images flashing across the screen. My favorite show was <u>Dragon-Ball Z</u>, yet the only time it seemed to be on Cartoon Network was when I had karate practice. Three times a week I went to practice, yet I progressed slowly. No longer did I have the drive that I had when I was younger. I was smarter than before and knew there was no way I could be a ninja. Yet somehow, I found myself wishing to be more than I was. Like the characters on my favorite TV show, I wanted to have powers to fly, to fight, and to be strong. But, more importantly, I wanted to be accepted.

Though my mind had the determination, my body did not. I would much rather sit in front of the TV dreaming than go outside and try to get in shape. My brothers always got the newest gaming system, beginning with NES, then SNES,

Nintendo 64, etc. Since these were *their* gaming systems, I could only sit and watch *them* play. However, I didn't really mind. I was content in letting my body and brain turn into mush, lying around doing nothing all day. Karate was just a hassle. So I quit. It was great for the first few weeks! Now I could watch all the cartoons to my heart's content. I loved my life, for I never had any obligations that wasted my precious television-time!

…Then came middle school.

"My name is Mrs. King," my teacher's voice sounded as she wrote on the chalkboard. A small wart on her nose seemed to grow larger the longer I looked at it. "You are no longer in elementary school, so I expect each of you to act your age." Kids my own age filled the room; almost all of them had neat little notebooks and binders. Listening intently, some of the kids even seemed to be writing down what Mrs. King was saying. I had a few blank sheets of paper out, but I could care less about what my teacher had to say. Instead of listening or taking notes, I doodled some pictures of cartoon characters that I created. Some day, I would be considered cool. I just never knew when that would happen.

After about an hour, the bell rang. I looked around and saw everyone getting up. "Strange," I thought, "recess can't be here already." I was still unfamiliar with having multiple teachers, so I got lost while trying to find my next class. I walked in a few minutes late.

"Nice of you to join us," said my teacher in an arrogant, acerbic tone. I felt blood rush to my face as I hurried and sat down in an empty seat. I sat back in my seat, wishing that I were invisible, feeling a class full of strangers beat me down with their piercing stares. "Like I was saying before being interrupted, my name is Mrs. Pollard and I will be your music teacher."

My day continued in much the same way—trying my best to hide from others. I don't think I said any word other then "here" to answer for roll call. When my final class ended, I bolted out of my seat to the spot designated to meet my brother Jacob so that we could walk home from school together. I waited for him there.

And I waited.

Finally, I got tired of waiting. It seemed that he had forgotten about me. Slowly, I walked home the one and a half miles, annoyed at the long walk. When I finally got there, no one was home. I found out later that my mom had taken Jacob to find me, but I got home before they did. So I plopped out in front of the television and turned on some Cartoon Network. There was nothing good on, but just the act of sitting and watching somehow eased the bitter resentments I felt towards school and life. There is nothing more numbing than cartoons to a school-age boy. And so I sat and watched, and it became a habit.

Some choices we make have a way of getting back at us in the end. Who would have thought that watching a couple hours of TV after school could create such a character flaw? Everyday after school, I would turn on some cartoons. If my parents got mad at me and made me go to my room, I would get angry and have a temper tantrum, acting out both physically and emotionally. Nevertheless, I had to listen to my parents because they were in charge of my well-being. However, homework was the last thing on my list of priorities. I would go to my room and play my Gameboy, listen to music, or just sleep, letting my imagination take over my body.

I never did badly in school, *per se*. I got A's and B's for the most part, especially in elementary and middle school. Homework wasn't emphasized as it should have been then. However, starting in 6th grade my grades began to drop in the classes that required some work. I did fine on tests (for the most part) because I have always had a good memory. However, my social studies grade dropped to a 60% as did my math grade. As those grades continued to drop, my parents finally started getting after me, making me do my homework, though I still didn't have the desire.

In 7th grade, the same thing happened in the same classes—math and social studies. But this time, my counselor who knew that I was in the gifted program and that there was no excuse for such a drop in grades caught me. My counselor, Mr. Braden, called me and my parents in for a meeting.

"Mr. and Mrs. Hobbs, your son's grades in his social studies and math classes have dropped significantly over this past grading period." I sat back, not caring about what my counselor had to say. I did fine in school—do a couple of bad grades really matter? When was I ever going to use social studies or pre-algebra in my life? I was going to be a cartoonist or programmer, maybe even a firefighter, so who really cared about middle school classes? However, my counselor went on. "Sam has the capability to do great things. He is gifted and talented. He just needs the motivation."

I sat for a second thinking about what Mr. Braden had said. No one had ever told me that they believed in me, except for those people in my immediate family. But this was coming from someone who only saw my schoolwork, who also saw others' work and could judge me against them. His statement gave me some self-confidence, something I had been lacking all of my school-aged life.

I was struck by Mr. Braden's words, but something else caught my attention: the look on my parents' faces. My mom looked as if she was ready to cry, a look of disappointment and grief all caused by my immature actions. My dad, who was usually stern when I got in trouble, had a change in his countenance. It was of sincere concern, not of anger or hostility. At that moment, I realized that my parents weren't there to make my life miserable. They were there to help me to be the best that I could be. And I knew that I was letting them down by being resistant to their guidance. Their restrictions were out of love, and I was turning it away as something of naught. From that day forward, I made a promise to myself that I would never be the one to cause my parents to be disappointed in me. I would be the best student; I would be the best son.

Every day after school, I told myself that I could not sit around watching TV. I started making lists and setting priorities. Always on the top of my priority list was to do my homework. I found that if I got right to it, it didn't take more than an hour at most. Many days, I could even finish my work in fifteen minutes.

When I started to do the simple task of working on my homework everyday, I found miracles come up in my life. Not only did I do my homework, but I also started to enjoy it. The more I learned, the better I became at communicating with others and in carrying on a real conversation. The more I worked, the better my grades became. In fact, the second semester of my 7th grade I started to get straight A's, and I have only had two Bs since then (one in 8th grade and one in 11th grade). And, as my grades got better, the happier my parents were. If that were not reward enough to keep my grades up, my parents often celebrated by allowing me to buy something, such as a game that I desired.

In seventh grade, I also began to play the viola. I practiced everyday, and since homework never took me too long, I practiced for considerably long periods (to the annoyance of my entire family). I used the same method of initiation that I used with my homework. I set playing my viola as a priority, so I practiced and started to enjoy learning how to read music and hear songs come together. It was my satisfaction to progress and play increasingly difficult songs. I practiced so much, in fact, that I didn't have time to watch TV, and I was no longer tempted into wasting hours in front of it. Music was my new hobby, no matter how much that annoyed my parents. Because of my diligence in practicing, by my first year of high school, a short two-and-a-half years of playing, I had made New Mexico All-State Orchestra.

The added benefit of my endeavors was that I was snacking less and more active, especially because I enjoyed playing basketball. The summer before my eighth grade year, I spent much of my time playing my viola and spending time outdoors shooting hoops. Because I was more active, I was burning more calories. I also hit my growth spurt. Within one year, I had grown what seemed like 8 inches and had gained little weight. I was a new person. I had more friends, I was more social, and I had talents that I could share with others. How much change a little work over an extended period of time can create!

In one meeting with a concerned counselor in middle school, I transformed myself from a low self-esteemed, overweight, lazy person into an outgoing, confident, and talented youngster. Now is the time you may be asking yourself, "Why did you drop out of high school?" Sometimes things don't go the way we plan. Life is full of unexpected twists and turns. But whatever challenges we are faced with is unimportant. Everyone has different challenges and different weaknesses. It is about how we overcome those challenges that really matters.

Some may say they cannot do something because they are not talented in a certain area. I say that they are just making an excuse. Take a concert violinist, for instance. Is he talented because it is in his genes? I assure you that he would not be where he his now because of luck. He started early and was determined. Now take a young person who hears this violinist and wants to become like him. This young person may believe he cannot do it, that he is not talented enough. Is this any excuse?

Say the young person begins to play, hears how bad he sounds, and gives up. What does this prove? The ones who excel to the top are those who do not give up; they are those who continue to practice despite the odds.

I was an average youngster, probably giving my parents a great deal of stress. In my adolescent years, I always tried to fit in but couldn't find the way. I started moving closer to my friends and further from my parents. You parents out there probably know what I am talking about—adolescents are hard to control. I never did anything truly "bad," however, because I still believed in the principles that I was taught at home and in church.

Not wanting to be scolded by my parents, I would always try to hide what I did wrong. To help demonstrate this, let me backtrack to the time that I was around three years old. Being curious about the world and what made things work, I would perform experiments without my parents' knowledge. One of these experiments took place on a Sunday afternoon in my parents' room, after returning home from church.

Earlier that day, I saw my mom turn on the lamp next to her bed. Electricity is amazing, especially to someone as young as I was. I noticed that in order for the lamp to work, it had to be plugged into an electrical outlet. In addition, when the lamp was plugged in, it would light up the room. I came up with a hypothesis: If the lamp lights up when plugged into the outlet, then I could light up if I was plugged into the outlet. It was *so* simple!

After we got home from church, and while my parents were busy in the kitchen, I sneaked into their room. I went through my mom's drawer and found what I was looking for: a small bobby pin. It was perfect. Slowly I walked towards the outlet, making sure that no one was coming. I stuck the bobby pin into the outlet.

I watched my opposite hand to see if anything was happening. To my great dismay, I did not start to glow. But I was so sure! How could this be? As I watched, I took a deep breath and for some reason smelt the acrid scent of burning flesh. I looked down at my hand on the bobby pin, and it had started to smoke. Sparks were coming out of the outlet. I let out a little cry and tried to drop the bobby pin, but I could not. It was as though some force was holding it there.

After a few moments (though it seemed like forever at the time), I dropped the bobby pin and ran off to the kitchen, trying hard not to let my parents know what had happened. I discovered that my dad had just burned his hand on the stove and was running the burned area under cold water. I looked at my finger and saw that it was black. It was throbbing and burning, so I ran to the bathroom and started running it under cold water until dinnertime.

Still, my parents did not notice. However, when my parents went to their room later that evening, they found a strange melted spot on their carpet. It was black and in the shape of a bobby pin. Reaching down through the carpet, they found the bobby pin. But who was the culprit?

My parents came to my room and asked me if I had stuck the bobby pin into the electrical outlet. I told them no, my head hanging low in shame. They asked to see my hand, and I had no choice but to show them the burn mark, which oddly had two prongs across my forefinger and thumb. They knew I had done it, but no matter what they would say, I said that I had not. My parents thought this was funny, but I had never been so ashamed. I was not punished, but I learned an important lesson through experience.

I continued to feel shame and embarrassment through my early years when I did something I knew my parents would disapprove of. I would try to hide when I did something wrong, yet my parents had a way of finding out that it was me.

In middle school, after I had made the mistake of lying to my parents and being severely scolded, my mom came into my room to talk to me, to give me one of those lectures that parents are so famous for. However, this one was different. "Sam, if you do something wrong, just tell us," my mother said in a kind and loving voice. "We won't get mad if it was an accident. You just need to tell us the truth."

I remembered what my mom told me a few weeks later. In our home, we have always had the rule of "No throwing a ball inside," which seems obvious since you can easily break valuable items. However, I had recently received an amazing gift for my birthday: a rubber ball attached to an elastic string, which could then be attached to one's wrist via Velcro. I had hours of fun playing with this ball outside and with friends. I noticed that one of my friend's moms let us play inside, and we didn't break anything. Was it harmful, then, to throw it inside our house?

When my mom wasn't home, I would take this ball and practice throwing and catching in my room. When I went to the kitchen, I took it with me. When I went to my parents' room to watch television, I took it with me.

On one occasion, I took the ball into my parents' room while watching some Saturday morning cartoons. By then, throwing and catching the ball was habit, so I thought nothing of it. However, I stood up during a commercial and threw the ball a little too hard. It came back at me angled upward, hitting the light fixture on my parents' ceiling fan. One of the three fixtures, a southwest-style turquoise and brownish-pink ceramic, broke into multiple pieces and fell to the floor.

Upon seeing this, I almost broke into tears. I knew that my parents told me not to play with the ball in the house, and I had broken their rule. Sure, it was an accident, but it was an accident caused by a transgression of the rules. However, remembering the words of my mother, that I shouldn't lie to her and hide my accident, I took the pieces and sought her out.

My mom looked a little disappointed, but seeing the sadness in my eyes, she told me that it was all right and that she would just replace the fixtures. She trashed the broken pieces. "It was just an accident," she reassured me, giving me a warm hug. Nothing more was said about the light fixture after that.

Was it wrong for my mother not to scold or punish me for my mistake? Was my mom promoting behavior that went against her own rules? No; my punishment was in my conscience and in seeing the disappointment in my mother's eyes. She didn't seem angry or upset. It was as if she was telling me, "This is why we have rules, no matter how silly they may seem." I never wanted my parents to be ashamed of my behavior. I never threw a ball in the house again.

Oftentimes teens are stereotyped as rebellious, and I wonder if this is really the teen's fault. Sometimes, it may be the result of improper parenting. I have never been a parent, but I have been a son and a teenager, and I believe that rebellious teens often feel neglected or confined.

Teens that are neglected may come from a family with many children, with some children who are more dependent on their parents than the others are. Because of neglect, unintentional as it may be, the teen will start acting out because of a need for some kind of attention. I have many friends who seem to be suffering from this problem, yet they are unwilling to admit it. The worst result I have seen is a pattern of habitual lying.

Confined teens are those who are given too many strict rules to follow. They feel that they have no independence, that they can't do anything they desire without dire consequences. Can you blame them? When expected to adhere to such extreme conditions, teens tend to spite their parents and break the rules deliberately.

When given too many rules, teens may also progress slower than usual. Yes, younger children need discipline and structure, but once they hit adolescence, they need to increase their independence. They can only learn from their mistakes if they make mistakes, and soon they will watch others and start learning from the mistakes of others. If my parents had given me strict rules when I was an adolescent, I wouldn't have felt comfortable going to them if I had problems or concerns. I would be afraid of castigation from my parents. However, I learned that my parents were my advocates and that I could trust going to them in times of need, even if I did something that I knew would disappoint them.

What is the perfect amount of attention a teen needs? I don't think that is a possible question to answer here in this book. There are too many factors, it would take too long to explore, and it really doesn't have anything to do with my life. I would just like to say that my parents did a wonderful job. They patiently put up with my shenanigans. They have lovingly guided my actions, not giving me a list of rules or expectations, but by living by example. Ever since the rubber ball incidence, I knew that my parents really did care for my wellbeing. They weren't just trying to find new ways of torture. They were trying to make me into a great individual, someone who can ultimately make a difference in the world.

There's one other point of parenting I would like to touch on. Too many parents want to mold their children into themselves. Is that the point of parenting? I think that parents should help their child become a good-standing citizen who is uniquely individual. Rules are nice, but they should be flexible and allow children to learn about and understand the world. I guess that's the way I see it. It annoys me when I see parents trying to control their children's lives, or when they are overly protective, or when they are overly lenient. Kids need boundaries. It helps them know that their parents care. However, everything is needed in moderation. Even good things can be bad if we have too much.

FOUR

*Y*OU *may think I am "Crazy-go-nuts" as Sloaner might say, but yes, I am writing the "lost" journal entry here in this funny-looking green-spiral notebook thingy. Well, hopefully I will get a nice hard back one tomorrow. I was reading though my old journal entries today and I realized that much has changed since last year: now, 9th grade is my best year. Yes, I have friends, followers, and a heck load of girls. "How?" you might ask, have I done this in such a short period of time. The answer is simple. I followed the advice of my first journal and didn't become a bum over the summer break!*

I was outside almost the whole time, getting a nice, dark, amazing tan that has, since then, turned yellow. Plus, I also started to lift weights (finally!) and now I am buff, but not just that, I'm ripped! I even have a band with a bunch of LDS friends. We are Unzipped! Along with the band and the body come many girls. The bad thing is, I'm not sure if they really like me as a crush or a friend. That really sucks. Oh well, though, they are all good.

Another thing I found that has changed is the sports I play. You see, I used to love, cherish, and almost worship basketball, but since coming to high school, I am now a wrestler. Yup. That means EVEN MORE GIRLS! But, they are all slutty and nasty, so they aren't my type. But wrestling is the best sport. It is so fun, challenging, and you get such an awesome workout! Since the summer, I have lost 30 lbs from wrestling. I now weigh 152 and might be able to go down and compete at 145. Yes, I think I will.

So, finals are next week Thursday and Friday (the 18th and 19th), and I am not looking forward to them. I am in a wrestling tournament on Friday and Saturday and my cousins are coming to town late Saturday. That will be fun.

Well, I see all those game codes at the front of this spiral notebook. Believe me, I am not like that any more. In the past couple of months, I have actually purchased a free weight bench, an Olympic bar, a curling bar, adjustable dumbbells, and much more. It is so convenient to have a free weight gym in your own back yard.

I am also making money now. I convinced my parents to let me have $10 a week, but I have to pay for almost all of the things I get. That's all right because at least I have money. I got a job from a photographer in our ward that started with mowing his lawn. After I mowed his lawn, we started talking, and I got a job to carry around his cameras at weddings and be his "photographer's assistant." Later, he hired me to edit his photographs [on Adobe Photoshop], and now that is my recent job. I take his pictures and tweak them for good money. The last picture I did (I was paid 20 bucks) was of President Hinckley who came to our regional conference. I had to take a man completely out of the background. But, now it looks awesome and is hanging in our [foyer]. Cool, eh?

Well, Christmas is coming soon, and the Lemmons [my cousins] are coming into town. I have decided to ask for a pocket pc again, but I don't really think I'll get one. Anyways, it's not about the presents that makes this time of year so special. It is the Holiday Spirit that floats in the air. We have decided to go caroling more often. That will be super fun. This month has also been super musical and busy for me. You see, today Dallin, Jacob, Justin and I sang "Ye Elders of Israel" in church. The reason why it was fun was because it was a cappella—four parts. We publicized it in seminary, telling everyone to come and writing it on the board. Britta came, Anne came, the Blackers came and left, and I think that is it for outside our ward. But, we did have a whole lot of people in sacrament meeting because of Brian's farewell. We did awesome. Now, I am practicing this duet "Guard Him Joseph" for next week, a duet with my mommy. The week after, I am playing a duet with Cameron, him on violin and me on viola. It is "Sheep may Safely Graze." That will be pretty cool.

With change comes an intrinsic amount of arrogance and pride. After starting high school, I lost my lazy habits and replaced them with egotism. It is funny how human nature forces us to take on habits, one in the place of another. To illustrate this, think of a chain smoker. If he is able to stop smoking, he is likely to get hooked on something else—chewing sunflower seeds, gum, or anything for that oral fixation. As it turns out, my habits were replaced with both good things and bad things.

On the one hand, I replaced being lazy with being productive. I turned myself into someone who was inimitably individual, someone with whom others could relate. However, with a new persona, I became infatuated with improving myself so that others would accept me. It's peer pressure, I tell you, it will get you every time. Ninth grade was an awkward shift from middle to high school. I was such a freshman that I don't know why seniors didn't jump me that year*. I thought I was cool, and I thought that being rowdy and rebellious would draw others to me. How wrong I was!

Pride in what we do is a necessary part of life, and I am not condemning it. But, when that pride goes over the top, it can become destructive. There is ALWAYS someone in the world whose achievements exceed our own. If we get too prideful and forget this important fact, we become defensive and refuse to admit that we are wrong (what I like to call the "know-it-all disease"). Pride can ruin relationships. It can destroy the ties of friendship and love.

I learned my lesson of pride through many life experiences. One of these experiences happened not too long ago, during the summer of 2006. You see, I am currently enrolled in a nursing program to become a licensed practical nurse. Throughout last summer, we had long days working in various hospitals with patients. One of the hospitals we worked at was the Women's hospital, spending time in the post-partum unit. Now picture this—a sixteen-year-old boy working with women and their newborn babies in the post-partum unit. It was bound to be uncomfortable. Yet, for some strange reason, I found that I loved working on this particular unit, especially in the newborn nursery.

One day, I was assigned to do the blood work for a beautiful little girl, only a few hours old. After checking her ID band with her mother's, I wheeled the infant off in her bassinet without really checking to see if I had all the necessary supplies. When I got to the newborn nursery where the blood draw was supposed to take place, I realized that this little girl did not have a blue bulb-syringe with her. These bulb-syringes are a requirement in the hospital since the young newborns can't effectively clear their airway by coughing. Here was my dilemma: keep my pride and risk the child having an accident, or lose my pride and lose major points off my clinical grade.

For those who know me, one of my greatest prides is in my academics. I never settle for less than the best. If someone I know gets a higher grade than I do in a class, I will go to the extreme in working and rising above them. This situation might have been easy for someone else, but I had no clue of how I should manage my present circumstances. Thoughts raced through my mind: "Oh great! My teacher will surely take major points off for patient safety!" I contemplated whether I should bring it up, leaning towards the "maybe she won't notice" side of the argument.

However, I finally sucked up my pride and, with my heart racing and a flushing feeling running through my face, I told my instructor that there was no bulb-syringe. My instructor looked a little frustrated, especially because we were running late as it was, but she went away to find a syringe. I waited near the infant for her to return.

And I waited.

After a good five minutes had past, my teacher finally returned with the new syringe, and we promptly went to work to draw blood and get the tests done. "We need to hurry and get started," she stated impatiently. "I guess the nursery staff forgot to restock their bulb-syringes when they ran out, so I had to run down to the clean utility room to find some more. Sorry for the wait." I held the infant's foot above her head while I did a heel stick and started to milk the area to stimulate blood flow. As I worked, I noticed a strange sound coming from this little baby girl. I looked over at her face, and she was already starting to turn blue.

She was gagging, trying desperately to breathe, yet something happened to be blocking her airway. I quickly sat her upright and reached for the bulb syringe. With one hand, I opened her mouth, and with the other, I used the syringe to suction her airway. I suctioned for about a minute, and the fluid that came out just didn't seem to end. Soon, a brown fluid started coming from her mouth, probably an amniotic fluid she had breathed in, or aspirated, at the time of birth. However, with the simple act of having a bulb-syringe readily available, I was able to remove the fluid from her mouth and throat without any permanent damage to the newborn.

If I had hidden the truth from my teacher, who knows what could have happened. Since it took so long to find the syringe, the infant may have sustained permanent brain damage or even death. It was only by swallowing my pride that I was able to prevent such a fate for an innocent little girl. I think this is a good example of Murphy's Law: "Whatever can go wrong, will go wrong." This is not being pessimistic. It is taking advice from a wonderful organization known as the Boy Scouts of America, whose motto just happens to be "Be Prepared."

I have found that when I have excess pride in my life, it is hard to be prepared for what may happen. Pride is like a blinder that will only allow an individual to see his or her own point of view. It is just like going back to being a toddler, when all one can see is himself, when all one can say is "Mine!" Part of being successful and living a quality life is seeing a situation from another's point of view than your own. Try to think back on the last argument you had. Did you look at that situation from the other person's point of view, or would your pride not allow you to do so, even when you were clearly wrong in that debate? Alternatively, if you were right, did you notice that the other person refused to see your point of view, only hearing what they wanted to hear?

Pride is a visor, forcing one to be egocentric and bigoted. But what does it accomplish? In small amounts, it may be useful to help with one's self-esteem and confidence. Maybe that is what pride was originally intended for. But when in excess, you can see it does not accomplish that purpose. Does an argument boost your confidence? I know it does not boost mine. Does it help you build closer relationships? In my experience, I have only seen friendships torn apart. Can you think of anything positive that comes from having excess pride, arguing, getting defensive, and not listening to others? No? Neither can I.

...I think that lowering our pride and becoming humble is something that we can all work on, no matter our age or status in society. I know that I have come a long way, but I still struggle often, even when I have it in my mind that I will be better. I am continuing to work on it, and how great would it be if everyone else did as well. Without pride, the world would be an amazing place. Oh well...I guess I'm just dreaming...

* I was jumped once, even though it wasn't by seniors, and I don't think it was due to pride. They were older, yet probably more immature even than I was. It was on March 7, 2003 when I was in eighth grade:

Men Accused Of Punching Teen

Boy Was Walking Home From School

BY CHRIS RAMIREZ
Journal Staff Writer

He didn't look too tough, wearing glasses and lugging a violin case.

Now, two Albuquerque men are facing felony charges of roughing up the 13-year-old boy in broad daylight.

A day of boozing and smoking marijuana ended with Steve Alderete, 24, and Michael Vargas, 19, going to jail, police said.

The pair were arrested Friday afternoon at Alderete's Tierra Antigua NE apartment complex, according to a criminal complaint, filed in Metropolitan Court.

The youth with the violin was walking home from Eisenhower Middle School when he was stopped by a man in a black sweatshirt near Juan Tabo and Eubank, the complaint said.

The man asked the teen where he lived and where he was going, but the teen said he wasn't going to answer, the document said. The man then punched the boy in the eye and knocked him out, according to the complaint.

When the boy regained consciousness, his glasses were missing. He also had a swollen black eye.

An off-duty officer saw two men running into a nearby apartment and directed police there. An officer knocked on the door, and Alderete answered, smelling of alcohol, the complaint said.

Vargas came to the door moments later, and both men were arrested.

Vargas, accused of punching the boy, initially gave officers a fake name. They doubted him, because he said he was 17 years old but gave a 1984 birth date, the complaint said.

Vargas and Alderete told police they had been drinking and smoking marijuana before the incident, it said.

At least one of the suspects blamed the victim, saying the youth was the aggressor.

Vargas told police the teen initially approached him and tried to hit him with the violin case after he asked the boy for the time.

Vargas told police he punched the teen out of anger because the youth yelled a swear word at him.

Vargas is charged with child abuse and larceny. Alderete faces two counts of conspiracy to commit a third-degree felony and contributing to the delinquency of a minor.

Their bonds were set at $7,500 each.

Article by Chris Ramirez
Publication: Albuquerque Journal (Albuquerque, NM)
Publication Date: 11-MAR-03

3-7-03

Well, it started as a normal day, but it was much more than that. I went to school as usual. After school was when my day changed. Shawn and I were walking home. Almost to the park near my house, a 19-year-old came up to us and started asking us questions like: where did you come from? Where do you live? We didn't answer. We tried to walk past, but he wouldn't let us. So, I held my viola case up and tried to push past him. He threw a HARD punch into my cheek and I blacked out for a few seconds.

When I opened my eyes, I was kneeling on the ground, searching for my glasses (which fell off my face), and people were starting to gather around us. Someone saw it happen and helped me out. They called the cops and everything. My cheek was REALLY swollen. My mom arrived a while later. They found where the men lived (there were two of them, one on a bike a ways away). So, they arrested them.

A bunch of my friends who walk home came to me, comforted me, told the police about me, and all of this. The men told a lie, but there were enough witnesses to prove them wrong. So, Zach stayed with me and my mom. We went home. But, we had to drive to the police station to give our statements and everything. They also took a whole bunch of pictures of my injury. We never did find my glasses, though everyone looked. It was pretty exciting. The policemen at the station were really funny and nice. The men [my assailants] were 24 and 19 years old and were handcuffed to bars. I hope we can get some money to replace my glasses and maybe even get me a palm-pilot and braces. That would be nice...

We then went home. My face was turning colors by then. We ate dinner then left for Merry Makers. Instead of going, Jacob and I stayed at Grandma's house, played cards, talked, listened to music, and played on the computer. It was fun. By then, my face was blue, red, and really swollen. Then we watched Just Married. It was really funny, but I had to sit close because of my glasses. We went home and said prayers. Now my cheek is dark purple and my eye is really bloody. Oh well.

FIVE

WRITING in a journal was one of the best things that I did in my early years. When I first started, it got a bit tedious because I decided I had to write a full-page everyday so that my life would not be lost. Looking back on that, I realized how impossible of a goal that was. It is nice to have a day-to-day account of my life, but when am I seriously going to sit down and read three hundred pages of, "I went to school, and it was the same as usual." Blah, blah, blah.

I think that this is the reason I stopped writing for a couple of years: I lost the dedication to the preservation of my memories. However, I found my journal when I was a junior in high school and realized how useful it could be, especially for my future posterity. Instead of writing every day, I started writing every week, every month, whenever convenient. Maybe that aspect of my character I inherited from my mom. I found that if I did a greater stretch of time, I could pull out the information I found to be interesting or important, and I could add commentary to my actions.

It was by reading through my journal and seeing how immature I was that I first started to make goals and set paths to reach them. I started to organize my life, giving up the credo of: Just go with the flow. In order to stand out, I had to find who I was; I had to become something great.

Noticing that I tended to stress out and breakdown if I saw how much work I needed to do, I started taking one day at a time. Scratch that—I started taking one *thing* at a time. Sure, I had a lot to do, but what does that matter? It was my goal to get through just one task, the thing that I thought was most important.

For the first time in my life, I bought a planner. What a simple yet profound invention! Whenever something came up in my life, whether it was a doctor's appointment or a homework assignment, I would immediately jot it down in my planner. It was not enough just to write things down, I soon found. I had to pull my planner out frequently throughout the day and conscientiously plan my activities. This is what I like to call *time management*.

31

In my mind, I prioritized the lists produced in my planner. Was studying for a test more important or working on a project? The answer usually came by what was coming up first, or what was worth more points, or even in which class I had a lower grade. My priorities set, I now started the work.

Before I started to make lists, I was always a procrastinator. What was tomorrow for if I have to work today? However, that soon changed as I worked down the list, getting my priorities done. Once I finished my day's priorities, I looked on to the rest of the week. Was there something else I could work on so that I wouldn't have to spend extra time later? If there was, I would start working, if even for ten or fifteen minutes. Sometimes starting the work is the most difficult part of a job.

After I finished my work and felt comfortable with what I had accomplished, I used the rest of my time for myself. I could read a nice book, play my viola, work out on some weights, or even play games. But, I never did any of those things unless I felt comfortable about my completed assignments.

As my high school years rolled on and more work started piling up, I realized that my method actually worked for larger loads. Some of my friends who looked into the incomprehensible jumble of my planner immediately became stressed—and it wasn't even their workload. However, I took one thing at a time, and what might have taken me a few days to accomplish took me only a couple of hours of hard effort. I took some breaks in the middle, believe me, but they were never more than fifteen minutes or I would lose the "homework mode."

I guess I'm just trying to say that the only way I progressed to where I am now was by organization and time management. Although my planner wasn't pristinely organized, it was in my head, and I knew my system. I planned my time carefully, and I set (and stuck with) my priorities.

1-4-04

...We had fun with the Lemmons, went to the aquarium, so on and so forth. For Christmas, I got: a pocket pc!!! It is an HP IPAQ. It's awesome! On New Year's Eve, we finally got DSL internet. Oh yeah.

We took Vernon to the doctor. I waited around for five hours. Finally, we came home. My face had been clearing up, but I still had some red, so my mom put some foundation on my face, and I was glad because it was a combined stake dance. Yup. Ours and East Stake. But, this dance was not like that Halloween dance written in my last journal. It was awesome. I dance every dance with someone different, only dancing with a few people twice (e.g. Britta, Courtney, etc.). It was four hours long. CRAZY!

What made this dance awesome was not the live band, or Unzipped performing, or being picked first in a girls choice song (snowball style), or sleeping on a table on the stage, or the snow cones, or popping balloons, or dancing with a balloon with a picture of a girl and a name on it, or that girls swarmed to me everywhere I went. It was that Sean came up to me and talked to me (multiple times) and she sat next to me. I asked her to dance the first song of the New Year. We dance, and talked, and laughed, but she didn't let me dip her. Too bad. But, afterwards, I hugged her instead. We both walked back to our groups, our groupies waiting. I saw Sean talking excitedly to them. Hope it was something good. I'm sure it was.

On the first, we went to Utah, walked around BYU, went swimming, lifted weights, bought BYU merchandise and a CTR ["Choose the Right"] ring, went shopping, got set in the dorms, dropped Jacob and Jess off, cried, and drove home.

1-1-06

It is a new year, and I decided I should probably continue in my journal. While reading my old entries, I realized how much I have changed. I was prideful and worldly. I was obsessed with girls. Well, no more! Well, not as much, at least. So let's fill in some of the big events I missed up until now.

I've been getting straight A's through high school with my Heavenly Father's help, I went on some amazing back packing trips, I got my Eagle Scout, and school this year has been incredibly hard. I'm in a nursing program until 6:30 pm every night and am dying! I want to become a surgeon (not sure of any specialty yet, maybe ER). Let's see, I weigh 190 lbs (the most ever!) but my strength has increased with it, and I am a Priest (sweet 16 and never been kissed; actually, never been on a date...). I have no life! I gave up my life this semester for school—the best grades in some of the hardest classes. I've done very well so far, but I really have no social life. I am currently contemplating getting a life this next semester, but I really don't want to sacrifice my grades. My philosophy is that I will have plenty of time after my mission and in college, so what's the hurry? I want scholarships and I want to be great, helping people, saving lives, and living the gospel. I stopped wrestling and stopped playing in orchestra to fulfill my goals.

It has been extremely difficult, but if I make it through, I'll have my nursing license (LPN) right out of high school, and I'll be making (hopefully) 20 dollars/hour. Now don't get me wrong—I still like girls. I just haven't made the time to go on any dates, and I try not to obsess about girls anymore. The New Year's dance was last night, and it was very fun. I continue to enjoy dance—break dance, ballroom, swing, etc. It's somewhat embarrassing, though, because I'm always dripping with sweat by the end.

Oh yeah, I went on Accutane last school year and my skin is doing much better. I still have small breakouts, but nothing major. To sum it all up: I love my life. It is difficult and challenging, yes, but I am all the better for it. I am excited for this new semester. I will get the best grades I can without killing myself. Hopefully I'll lose a little weight while I'm at it...

Six

I love my life. I know you, whoever may be reading this in the distant future, may think my life is dull and monotonous, filled with nothing but studying and school, and for the most part, you are absolutely right! However, there are moments that I live for.

For the moment, I am bored out of my mind. I don't know what to do. It is Thursday evening, I took my midterm for pharmacology and did fairly well (89%; 91% after two questions were thrown out), and I am absolutely sick of studying. So, I am writing.

This was a wonderful week, and that's saying something. I spent time in the newborn intensive care unit, and I watched a Cesarean Section. Cool. I have just started getting the hang of OB and now it's over! I am so sad that I'll have to go from changing newborns' diapers to changing old men's diapers again. Gross. Oh well, life often takes unexpected turns, now doesn't it?

I don't know if you knew this or not, but I had big dreams of becoming a surgeon. Through the nursing program, I started leaning towards anesthesiology. I found the C-section I watched on Wednesday (yesterday) to be incredibly awesome and I could see myself doing stuff like that, but to tell you the truth, it is not as appealing to me as it once was. Don't get me wrong. I think cutting people open or putting them to sleep would be incredibly cool jobs, but I have really come to enjoy working with newborns and kids. Don't tell anyone, but I am actually considering pediatrics or a related field just because it would be something I think I'd really enjoy. But, only time will tell where I will be in 20 years. Gosh! I'm only 16! That seems like an awfully long time to be in school...

During my obstetrical nursing rotation at the Women's Hospital, my instructor told me, "Sam, you're really great with kids. You should be a baby nurse.

Have you ever considered becoming an OB/GYN?" That would be kind of weird, let me tell you. However, I think I might just have to go into working with kids...

So let me tell you a bit about myself. My name is Samuel David Hobbs, born on July 15, 1989 at 9 lbs 8 oz. Big baby, eh? My Apgar scores were 8 and 9. I was born in Orem, Utah but have been raised in Albuquerque, New Mexico. I used to have extremely terrible acne, but after intensive treatment of Accutane and Retin-A, it is finally under control and I am more confident. I am 5' 11.25" and just want to reach that 6-foot mark! I love my family, my church, and my Heavenly Father. I love my life!

As evidenced by my early life, I have never really stuck with anything to the end. I quit karate before I reached my black belt level. I quit singing in choir before I entered high school. I quit playing the viola in orchestra before I made best in state. I quit wrestling before I made varsity. Lastly, I dropped out of high school with less than 40 school days before I graduated.

Some may call me a failure. But, to tell you the truth, I don't think I would change anything that I have experienced. Sometimes I regret not sticking with karate. I gained weight and became lazy. However, without those experiences, I could not look back now and learn from what I had done. At an early age, I learned that my decisions *now* will affect my overall well-being *later*. I don't know about you, but when I actually experience something, I learn more than just being taught. Take a simple fact of life: If you eat too much fat, you may have a heart attack.

"Hmm..." you may think, "I should cut back on my fat intake." What a marvelous idea! A simple lifestyle change from day to day can prevent an awful death by fat! But, such are fleeting thoughts, for when the smell of ground beef frying in oil drifts into your nostrils, your mouth starts watering, and your only desire is to take a bite of that juicy burger.

Twenty-five years down the line, you continue to listen to your senses. Who cares if fat causes heart attacks? It will *never* happen to me. As you walk out of your car, heading towards your office and stressing over an upcoming presentation, you feel a gripping pain in your chest. "It must be heartburn. I'm fine, perfectly healthy." Then your left arm starts going numb; you are out of breath, light headed, and sweating profusely; the stabbing pain in your chest gets worse. You feel your impending doom looming over your head. Your vision starts to fade; everything goes black.

You wake up in the hospital, an IV pumping fluids into your arm, strange noises and beeping from foreign equipment fills the room around you. A group of five or six residents then comes into the room, surrounding your bed, their hands tucked away into their large white lab coats. "What happened?" you ask.

"Well," the gruff older physician begins, "based on your current electrocardiogram, we diagnosed you as having an acute myocardial infarction. Luckily, we did not note any Q-wave present, but there is definitely ST elevation. Moreover, your cardiac enzyme levels have raised quite a bit, especially creatine kinase. You also have a mildly elevated troponin, indicating some congestive heart failure. Based on your diagnostics, we recommend a balloon angioplasty with the placement of a stent STAT. While you wait, we will continue your nitroglycerin drip to prevent any further vasoconstriction and infarction. You will also be getting diuretics to prevent hypertrophy of your myocardial muscles and respiratory distress from fluid volume overload."

"Was that English?" you think to yourself. All you can do is lie in your bed, waiting for who-knows-what to happen. Now let's say that a nurse enters your room, and in a matter-of-fact sort of way asks you about your pain level and your bowel habits. You think to yourself, "What does that have to do with anything?" You have lost your independence. You have lost your dignity. Luckily, the one thing you didn't lose was your life.

Now, let's say that your doctor comes into your room, getting ready to release you from the hospital. He hands you an order for outpatient medications, a list of twenty or so words that make absolutely no sense to you, whether due to their foreign complexity or the illegible writ in which they were scribbled. Your doctor then looks straight into your eyes until you feel squeamish as he says, "You need to cut back on your fat intake."

What is more convincing to your nutrition habits: hearing the simple fact that fat can cause a heart attack or living through the experience? When I decided to quit karate, I was only thinking about what I wanted now. I did not look at the overall detrimental effect that it would have on my health. However, as I saw my abdomen starting to grow, as my classmates began to ridicule me, and as I found myself to be physically challenged in simple tasks, I made an oath that I would not let it happen again.

You may be asking yourself: what does this have to do with quitting orchestra or wrestling? What knowledge was there to glean from quitting something that you were talented at and loved to do? I will answer those questions by saying that I never wanted to quit those activities. If it were possible, I would do everything that I enjoy. Time passes by too quickly to do everything we want to, especially in our younger years. However, I found that I wanted to make the most of my time. I evaluated my situation and made the difficult decision to drop many of my extracurricular activities.

The sport that I loved above all others once I entered high school was wrestling. I don't want you to get me wrong—I still love to wrestle. However, even though I am both challenged and have fun while competing, if I think of my future, I don't see wrestling as one of my priorities. Will I ever be a pro-wrestler? Maybe, but most likely not. One main benefit of wrestling was the workout that I was getting at the practices, but I realized that I can get a good workout going running for half an hour, or by jump roping, or by going swimming, or even by dancing, thereby saving me the time commitment of being on a team. I can still be active. By stopping wrestling, I was able to enroll in a nursing program every afternoon after high school, thereby enriching my academic achievements.

Dropping orchestra was difficult, plainly said. But, I had a great desire to further my education. As it turned out, my orchestra teacher moved our class from 0-hour to 6th period. This would be all fine and dandy if nursing had started later. However, my classes and clinical rotations started at 2:30 pm every day, the same time that orchestra would have ended. I don't know about you, but I find it difficult to travel fifteen miles instantaneously. Again, I evaluated my situation. Yes, I could go on and be a music major and performer. But was that what I wanted? In the end, I don't want to entertain people. I want to help them. I want to save lives. I don't think that orchestra would accomplish that goal I had set in my mind.

I still play my viola, and I still try to work on improving my talents and skills. Instead of performing often, I tend to play more for me. When I am having a particularly stressful day, I can start playing some Bach or Tchaikovsky, and immediately the stress dissipates into nothingness. This may sound selfish on my part, but I think that all of you can agree that sometimes we need time for ourselves, where we can get away from the fast-paced world of today.

You may be wondering: How can you expect to graduate from nursing if you drop out of everything you start to excel at? I don't want to be a nurse; I think all of my friends know that. Nurses get what I like to call the "dirty job" of the hospital. Of course, there is more than just disgusting tasks, but sometimes it does get dirty. Take, for example, an experience I had my junior year:

4/25/06

...Tuesday was especially difficult for me because of the patient to which I was assigned. He had a urinary tract infection, pneumonia, chronic renal failure, an above the knee amputation, and dementia. On top of that, he was incontinent of diarrhea. When I arrived, I realized how depressed this man really was. His code status was do not resuscitate/do not intubate, and he refused dialysis so toxins were building in his body. He also refused a medication that would lower his potassium because it caused his diarrhea incontinence, but he risked having a heart attack. There were other ailments and abnormal assessment findings, including a pain level of 10 out of 10, but I won't go into that now.

I spent hours in this patient's room talking, giving him a bed bath, getting him out of bed, etc. He was definitely confused, which, with depression, is depressing itself to see in a person. When I was taking his temperature, he held the thermometer like a cigarette. After trying to smoke it, he told me, "There's nothing in this one." At another point during our visit, he told me he thought he saw his car. He pointed to the "parking lot," which just happened to be his bed. He also conversed with the television in his room, asking the news anchors if they spoke Spanish.

My patient was on contact precautions because his infections were methicillin-resistant staphylococcus aureus (MRSA) positive, and his stool was positive for Clostridium difficile. That being said, I had one major disaster while changing my patient's diaper. He casually told me that it needed to be changed, and since my patient could stand, it should have been an easy diaper change. But it wasn't. When I took it off, I found that my patient had gone very little. However, right when I moved to put the new diaper on, my patient let loose the floods of Noah.

Luckily, I had my gown on to protect most of my clothes from the foul-smelling, soupy disaster. However, there was fresh stool all over the floor, my shoes and pants, and even on the wall. It was an emotionally difficult day, and my stress levels kind of peaked so that I couldn't really hold back some tears. My patient, on the other hand, did not move, smile, or open his eyes when I first came, but by the time I left, he looked into my eyes and gave me a heart-warming smile...

After reading that account, who would ever want to be a nurse? In the long run, I do not, though I have to say that changing a newborn's diaper is much more pleasant than changing an older person's diaper. Why, then, do I stick with it? How am I at where I am now, still enrolled in nursing, and ready to graduate in only two months? Anyone with "common sense" would have dropped already if they had been subjected to what I have been. Indeed, many have dropped and have been cut. There were over 200 applicants for the program in which I am enrolled. Of those 200, 50 made it to be in the junior class. Of those 50, there are 24 of us left on the path to graduation.

Why haven't I dropped out of nursing? I guess you could say I'm crazy. How I see it is that every experience is worth it. Like the one mentioned before, at the time I cried out of frustration, but now I can look back on that experience and laugh. Looking back on similar experiences, I know that if I can handle what I have, then I can handle anything. If I can take care of an 80 year old, one-legged, incontinent, dementia patient, then I can definitely take care of my children once I become a father. If I can be professional and proficient while replacing a prolapsed uterus in an elderly woman (and yes, that really did happen), then how much easier should it be to ask a girl on a date and keep my moral standards high?

How I see it, no matter what challenge we are faced with, if we overcome that challenge then we will be strengthened in other aspects of our life. That is partially why I am sticking with nursing. I want to become a doctor eventually, and I know that

I will be ahead of some of my peers who have similar aspirations because of the work that I am doing while I am young. I know how to handle myself in difficult situations.

Whatever field someone decides to go into, I can guarantee that there will be aspects of the job or training that will be discouraging to that individual. For me, I have decided that I really don't enjoy working with elderly people. Sometimes it is all right and I can enjoy the company of my patients, but, for the most part, it is not something I want to be doing for a living. However, I like certain aspects of nursing, especially working with pediatrics and with newborns. What can I say? I love babies! I also enjoy the end result of my labors, especially when I can tell that I made a difference, however small, in another's life.

6-28-06

On Monday I took care of a LOL (little old lady) who was on total parenteral nutrition (nutrients through an IV into the large vena cava vein) and had a nasogastric tube in. [A nasogastric tube (NG tube) is inserted through the nose into the stomach. In this case, it was on suction to relieve nausea]. She was tiny yet could not seem to put on weight. Two days earlier, she was at 81 lbs, and when I was caring for her she dropped down to 79.5 lbs.

This LOL told me that she was feeling really down. I noticed that her NG tube wasn't really draining any fluids from her stomach. I checked her NG tube and flushed it with air, and, in less than two hours, over 800 ml of dark, frothy green fluid came out. And, it continued to flow. Afterwards, she told me that she felt the best she had in a long time.

Later in the day when she was giving herself a sponge bath, her NG tube came loose. I tried to secure it but did not have extra tape. As I hurried out of the room to get some tape and my instructor, I saw that her NG tube had come completely out. I could not believe how extraordinary this woman was, because when I came back she had put the tube back in herself! I checked the placement and found that she had done an incredible job, so I secured the tube to her nose...

I was grateful on Tuesday to have the same patient. I wanted to learn more about her history and help her be comfortable, if possible. Much of what I did was the same as Monday, so I was able to provide care with more skill and efficiency. In administering medications, however, I almost forgot to verify the patient. I can never manage to not make mistakes! I hope that I will improve, however, and perfect the art of med administration by the end of the summer.

On Tuesday, I also had the opportunity to assist my patient in washing her hair, a difficult task without a hair washing basing, trying to maneuver around an NG tube and an ileostomy (drainage tube out of the small intestines, pouching out onto the abdomen). No wonder she had not had her hair washed since her admission! Finally, it was done, and my patient's countenance changed. She smiled more and beamed with happiness and gratitude. "I feel like a new woman," she said to me. I am just grateful that I could help...

My sister has currently been going through what I was when the poop disaster happened. She was re-thinking her plan of going into art education with only a semester to go. Part of her training was to teach classes of all different age groups. While working with some of the kids, maybe she got discouraged because she did not feel she could control the class. Maybe she didn't think that it was worth her time to be teaching these little brats who don't have any desire to learn. She told me that she didn't want to be a teacher, that she didn't enjoy what she was doing.

I think that teaching is one of the noblest professions, though definitely one of the most difficult. My advice to my sister was this: take each day one at a time, and don't over-stress about your work and your job. It is difficult when you think you want to do something and yet find the task almost unbearable. However, it is worth it to stick with it. If the problem you are facing is with elementary school kids, you now know that elementary school isn't where you should be. You may want to work in high schools where the students choose to take a class because they want to, where there is more discipline and longer attention spans (though there are different issues you will have to deal with).

If you find you can't stand teaching, no matter what the age group, it may be necessary to reevaluate your current plan and start working towards a different future. Whatever profession you choose to go in to, go through all the way with your education and training, and be patient while you work. All you need to do is find your niche.

My niche isn't working with older people, and I'm sure it never will be. However, I learned to love kids, and I enjoy making a difference in others' lives. That is where I feel I am destined to end up—helping children get better. But, as I grow, mature, and have a greater number of experiences, I might find my attitudes changing as well.

On Friday, March 16, 2007, my sister wrote in her blog, "A *major* change is about to occur in my life...any guesses? No, mom, I'm not pregnant! I'm changing my major! It's a little nutty considering that I am a senior, but I feel so good and excited about it. I've been doing Art Education K-12 for the past year now, and I've never been really pumped or passionate about it.

"This semester I was able to do a practicum class, which gave me the opportunity to teach by myself in actual classroom settings, and...I HATED IT! Ha ha! I taught 1st, 7th, and 8th grade, and it was an absolute wreck. My 1st graders went wild and the middle schoolers moaned and groaned all period long. Teaching makes me anxious and sick to my stomach, and I don't like being an authority figure. I decided to go a completely different direction and have decided to get a BA in English with an emphasis in creative writing and a minor in Art. I can't wait to start my classes this summer! Woo hoo!"

My sister ended up changing her major, though still wanting to use her creative juices to influence the lives of children. She is now going into English with the hopes of writing and illustrating her own children's books. I have always looked up to the person that my sister is. She is sweet, loving, and fun, and I know that whatever decision she makes will benefit both herself and others in the future.

SEVEN

...IT is now the summer of 2006, the infamous and dreaded has now arrived. I read back over my little "catch up" entry and realized that it all is still pretty much true. I no longer have straight A's, however, because this semester killed me. A's in everything except nursing. What a concept, huh? I realized, however, that one B will not ruin my future. High school grades don't matter after that first semester in college. And besides, what does one B mean? It means I am off the hook for giving a speech at graduation. Yay!

...This semester I have grown in strength of body, mind, and spirit. I have learned much about how to be a nurse...Oh yeah! I have officially been on three dates this semester. The first was a fun double date with Britta, this kid Matt, and his friend from the East Stake. We went "restaurant hopping" followed by hours of laser tag at Hinkle Family Fun Center. It was <u>CRAZY</u>! So fun! I would never guess the girls would enjoy it so much, but they did. We went out for ice cream afterward at McDonald's. I kind of felt bad because Matt paid for everything, which must have been <u>insanely</u> expensive.

So, my second date. Oh, by the way, the girls asked me for these first two. Good thing, because I probably would have been studying if it wasn't for them. Okay, my second date was a girl's choice dance (Winterball) at La Cueva (actually, it was held at the Convention Center). So, I got a nice suit at a thrift store and a black shirt and purple tie at Wal-Mart, purple to match my date's (Jenevera) dress. To ask me out, she put smarties and dumdums all over my car with a sign that stated, "Don't be a dumdum, be a smartie."

When I went to school, Jenevera, Whitney, and Justin were sitting against their lockers, right next to mine, which they did every morning. This time, however, Justin handed me a rose and asked me to Winterball, which was kind of creepy. Then,

45

Whitney said, "Don't be a dumdum, be a smartie." Then Jenevera asked me out. Cool. My locker was filled with candy, too. I feel kind of stupid now, though, because I just told her "Yes," I didn't do anything creative or nice. Oh well...

So, the dance was fun, though I have never seen any worse kind of dancing from high school students (bumping and grinding, it would be called). We had dinner before hand at Jessica's home (we went with a pretty humongous group). Afterward, we had ice cream at Jenevera's house. Yum.

Okay, so those two dates ended each about two in the morning and I had a pretty lousy clinical week afterwards. Do you think that "sleep" and "good grades" are related? But sleeping during school probably isn't the best idea... On my third date, I actually asked someone (well, actually multiple people) out. On Thursday evening, I got a call from Dallin wondering if I could double with him on Friday. I said yes, and then we had to decide what to do. We decided to make homemade pizza at my house then wing it from there, maybe ending with some salsa dancing.

I called tons of people Thursday night but got a hold of no one. Everyone had something going on! On Friday, I asked tons of people at school, but they were all going to parties or what naught. I went to nursing with no date and no idea who to ask. I didn't want to be a "third wheel," so during break, I called Dallin for a couple of phone numbers, one of which was Kirsten. I had called Kirsten as my first choice but only talked with her parents. I called her again at about 4 pm to ask her out that very same night at 7 pm, and guess what? She said yes!

That word has never sounded so good. So, that evening, Kirsten showed up first so we played some foosball. Dallin came with Sara and Bryan came with his girlfriend from the West Stake. We made two pizzas, played games, and enjoyed each other's company. Great fun. I kind of feel like a jerk, though, because Kirsten drove herself to my house and, after the date, I didn't even walk her to her car! I said goodbye at the door and that was all. Gosh! What was I thinking?

Now that all of that is over, let me say more about my life. I am finally a senior in high school! I am counting down the days to the end. It has all seemed so quick, yet I am having a difficult time believing that in a year it is all going to be done with and behind me.

So, going on. Nursing has taken over my summer. Last week was finals week. Monday I had three finals (my last classes as a junior) and three hours of lecture on newborns. Tuesday I had a test on postpartum and two hours of lecture. Wednesday I had my Newborn Test and five hours of lecture. On Thursday, I had my obstetrical nursing final and five hours of lecture. On Friday, (no tests, thank goodness!) I had seven hours of lecture. How boring!

Clinicals started this week, which means I have nine hours of hospital work Monday-Wednesday, lecture and tests every Thursday, and Fridays off. Yay [unenthusiastically]. On top of that, I have to read two books for English (Zorro by Isabel Allende, which I highly recommend, and Life of Pi by Yann Martel, which I haven't read yet) and finish up four correspondence classes (actually, get started on four correspondence classes). This week was fairly easy because Monday was Memorial Day, Tuesday was orientation, and Wednesday I went to the clinic (I gave my first "real" shot to a patient there, a Hepatitis B vaccine). Thursday I had a freakin' hard test on anti-infectives and five hours of lecture.

Today I decided to be lazy. I watched The Mask of Zorro, lifted weights, and played my viola (it has been so long; I forgot how much I love it!). Then I did only a little homework. Next week, I have two days of medical-surgical nursing and one day of newborn, followed by a test on gastrointestinal drugs. The week after I am starting OB (which I am not so happy about. Do you know how uncomfortable it is going to be being in a new mother's room, assess EVERY aspect of her body, and trying to teach her? Come on, I'm sixteen, how can I ask to feel her breasts or look in unmentionable places? What if her husband is there? Weird...). I also have a test on cardiac drugs and a take home test on anti-neoplastics, but I'm going to Zion's Camp next weekend so I have no idea of how I'm going to cram it in. Oh well, such is life. It will be worth it in the end, though the end seems forever away, and who knows what the future will have in store? I just hope there's no more explosive Clostridium difficile positive diarrhea all over my clothes or multiple diaper changes one after another.

It's getting kind of late, and I got tons to do tomorrow. Sorry if I bored you, this was a long entry, but I didn't want to leave any of the lovely details out (except for my plans to swipe a baby at newborn...).

6-10-06

As you have probably noticed, I tend to skip a few days every now and then. This is only because nursing is taking over my life, and if I have lots of paper work, I can't write, and if I don't have paper work, then I have a lot of studying for Thursday's test. Because you can read about clinicals in my clinical journal, I'll spare you the details.

I do want to say that on 6-6-06 (was the date just a coincidence? j/k), Tuesday of this week, I was able to go to the newborn nursery accompanied by my good friends Dayven and Sara, and yes, we did swipe a baby, though not out of the hospital because an alarm would have gone off. Instead, we went to a woman who only spoke Spanish, took her baby from her, and strolled the baby off to the newborn nursery, an illegal act because we are just students. Oops.

I have decided, however, that I absolutely love newborns. That is correct. They are so cute, small, and innocent; there is something about them that I can't get enough of. It's especially adorable when they suck on your finger or demonstrate plantar reflex by curling their cute little toes around your finger. I mean, who wouldn't love newborns? Since OB starts next week, I was very nervous and apprehensive, but now I am much more enthusiastic because I know I will be working with the newborns as well as the mothers. Cool. So anyways, that was my favorite clinical day <u>*ever*</u>*.*

On Thursday, I took a test over GI drugs, which was much easier than the test last week. One girl got 100%, two got 98%, and I got a 96%. Not bad for cramming in one hour the night before... That's bad; I gotta stop cramming. I could be doing so much better! But, because of the fancrapulously large stack of paperwork I bring home every night for my medical-surgical rotations, it doesn't seem like I have a choice.

On Thursday night after school, I went up to Zion's Camp. It took forever to get up because we got lost by not making a correct turn. We arrived at a little past midnight, and since I had been up since 4:30 am, I crashed. Friday was good fun, though it was not at all like last Zion's camp. Last time I was still a little cocky weird kid, so a majority of my time was spent shirtless, playing "13," and listening to music while sun bathing. This time I was almost the oldest one there. Weird. I missed the first day because of nursing, but the day I was there I did orienteering and the station my ward put on, namely sword fighting, playing "King of the Log" with pugil sticks, knife and hatchet throwing, and blowgun shooting. Now I am pretty darn good at throwing knives and shooting blowguns. Cool.

At Zion's camp, Brother Ames was in charge of making this ginormous tower modeled after King Benjamin's tower. Some called it the Tower of Babel. Others called it the Ramiumptum (me included) [Mormon joke]. It had to be at least 60 feet tall and was created entirely out of dead, fallen timbers and rope lashings. Bishop Hall gave a sermon on the top on Friday night, and every Bishop bore their testimonies at the top following him. Then, the rest of us had the opportunity to bear our testimonies. It was really great. I started feeling like I should go up, then I felt a solid jab into my side. Looking over, I saw the source was a long stick carried by Bishop Hall. What a funny man. Anyways, I did get up and shared my testimony.

On Saturday, we had our service project, which consisted of moving heavy logs into massive piles for burning. It was hard, but we finished. After lunch, and after swiping tons of chips, cookies, and doughnuts, we headed home. I finished writing a paper for nursing on the side effect of chemotherapy but did not study for my cardiac drug test next week. I really gotta crack down on that stuff...

EIGHT

...*ON Monday, July 31, we departed on our 50-mile backpacking trip. To sum it up, it was long, hard, miserable, yet satisfyingly fun and worthwhile. We all left on Monday morning with the bishopric and Brother Barnett to wave us off. The trail we started on began at 11,000 ft above sea level and went up to over 12,000 ft. The first day started all right, but before we knew it, we lost the trail: never a good thing. Skyline trail, the one we trekked for the main part of this hike, wasn't very well marked, to say the least. It would appear and disappear randomly, slowing our progress.*

Soon enough two groups naturally divided—a slow group and a fast group. The fast group consisted of me, Jacob, my dad, Andrew (aka "Patrick"), and Naegle. The slow group consisted (for the most part) of Allen, Dillon and his dad, Brother Davidson, and Brother Naegle. As the fast group traversed the barren wilderness, we started to go through a burnt forest (which might explain the lost trail). Slowly, we started heading down the side of the mountain, following my dad's GPS waypoints, instead of staying at the top (our first mistake). Whoever goes down must come back up, so after we headed up the mountain we were pooped. That's when the clouds started rolling in.

Instead of setting up a dinette fly, as we should have, we ran back to shuttle backpacks from weary travelers in the slow group. By the time everyone made it to the trail on the top of the ridge, it started to rain. Before I had time to grab my poncho, the rain turned into a wicked hailstorm with ice the size of large marbles, pelting us from above. It shredded ponchos, soaking all of our gear and us. We ran to the nearest shelter of trees and set up camp.

Jacob and I went to bed right away (it being just two in the afternoon). I read <u>Zorro</u> *while Jacob slept. After dinner, we again slept. On Tuesday, we stayed at camp the entire day. My dad and I went on a couple of water runs, and we found water exactly where the map said it would be—a little stream down a steep hill. After filling up tons of Nalgenes, my dad and I washed our hair in the stream. That felt so nice! However, the hike out was incredibly tough. We basically had to climb out of a cliff. Plus, more clouds were rolling in (not the menacing looking ones, thank goodness), which meant that there was crazy fog on the mountain so that I couldn't see twenty feet in front of me. Pretty scary when you don't know where your camp is.*

Anyways, we sat out Tuesday, went on a day hike, let our stuff dry, hunted with a sling shot, etc. We weren't even seven miles into our trip and we had people wanting to bail out! What the heck! On Wednesday, we headed out towards the camp we were supposed to reach on Monday. We made it. It was supposed to be at a lake, but none of us could find such a lake, so we settled for a nice little camping spot. It was a difficult day, however, with many ups and downs. We tried getting the slow guys up front to talk to them and keep them moving. It worked.

Being immediately after Youth Conference, this backpacking trip gave us a lot to talk about. We found that there are two things that really kept us moving—girls and food. Life is similar, ain't it? What else keeps us moving and on the straight and narrow? Anyways, I talked to Allen about his latest crush, a girl in the Eldorado ward (East Stake) named Leah (her parents were my chaperones at youth conference, though I don't think I've met Leah). To keep Allen moving, I told him that Leah was waiting for us at the Truchas Lakes, that I had called her on a cell phone to come meet us. It was funny.

While we walked, Allen and I planned Homecoming and a double date, both of which he was planning to ask Leah. Now, with Dillon I talked about Jenessa, though I did tell him that it was not my fault if something happened between us. I think he hates me now. :) He was somewhat angry with me but was forced to comply. She is a freshman and I'm a senior, but by the time I'm off my mission, she'll be eighteen. That's actually a pretty good match, doncha think? j/k.

As we hiked, we also planned a Zoolander party for Saturday night. I told Dillon (aka Baby D) that he could only come if he swam across Truchas Lake with me. I told him I'd be inviting Jenessa, so he was eager to make it to Truchas and swim across just to come to my party. Hehe, I'm so evil!

Naegle talked about Sandra, one of his sisters on the handcart trek last year. He hadn't seen her in a long time but planned on finding her number and asking her out. By the time Wednesday ended, we knew all about each other's crushes and were craving Blake's Lotaburger (Dillon's dad offered to treat us all if we made it, so we all fantasized about the amazing meal waiting for us).

By the end, we were all tired but needed to scope out a nice camp near water, so we continued. We planned on going up a little hill to camp, but one of the scouts kind of lost it. He threw down his walking stick and backpack and refused to move. We continued on up to set up camp without him, wanting to let him cool off before confronting him, but my dad got angry and kind of yelled at him. We got him to come up to camp, but he just sat on a log and refused to move. So, we went on a water run to let him cool off. We took our time so that by the time we got back, he was sitting next to the fire, still a little strung up. We continued being cool, playful, and friendly, and soon everything turned out all right. It did give us a little scare, however, because we were 20 miles into the mountains with no way out, and I certainly did not want to carry this certain scout on my back.

On Thursday, we continued on to Truchas. I forgot to mention that every day it rained, mainly at lunchtime. During these times, we whipped out a 10 x 10 foot tarp, set up a dinette fly, ate lunch, played "13," and sat out the storm. It was kind of nice, but cramped. Thursday was no exception. It is a little scary to be on one of the highest ridges in New Mexico during a lightening storm, lugging a backpack with a metal frame on your back. But, no one died, thankfully, though many of us came close. The lightening was incredible to experience from such a short distance—flashes of blue coming from all around, lighting up the sky with loud, lagging BOOMs.

Thursday was filled with tons of up hill, so talking became more important than ever. We planned more dates and added to the ones we already planned. I don't know how many of them will actually go through, mainly because I'm broke. We also talked about how nice our swim in Truchas Lake would be after all of this hiking. Most of the hike was through the clouds, so it was hard to see and crazy cold. But, we continued on our journey and made it. What a glorious sight, that amazing lower Truchas Lake!

Immediately after setting up camp, I was stupid enough to go through with my plan of swimming. Patrick and I were the first ones in the lake, swimming across only because we vowed we would. We were shaking; hyperventilating; and our feet, hands, and face had turned blue. What were we thinking? In addition, evil-looking clouds were rolling in, warning us to go back to the camp. But we didn't. Well, I didn't; Patrick did.

I got back in the lake with Baby D and Allen. (Can you believe I got Allen to get in? He threatened to kill me after the fact.) We washed our hair and bodies, and it felt so good! However, by the time we got out, we felt raindrops hit our exposed skin. We tried to dry off, throw our clothes on, and run back to camp, but it was too late. It started to pour, and we got drenched. I had also forgotten to put my pack cover on my backpack before I left, so most of my gear and extra clothes got drenched as well.

We stayed under tarps all night, used rainwater from the tarp to make hot drinks, and didn't eat dinner before going to bed. I threw on some of my dad's dry clothes to warm up, and my sleeping bag, to my great astonishment, wasn't too wet, so it kept me super warm (that was helped by the fact that it was a synthetic fill rather than down feathers). On Friday morning, we dried our gear out as well as we could, which isn't saying much. I had melted some K-Swiss tennis shoes trying to dry them by the fire, and I wanted to leave them on top of Truchas peak. Being unable to summit, however, I instead tied them together and chucked them into a tree.

As we headed out a little before ten, we decided that we didn't want to stay another night. Instead of going to Pecos Baldy Lake and setting up camp as we had planned, we kept on walking and hiked out on Friday. We made it to the cars by 6:30 pm. Still, it was a lot of walking, a lot of talking about girls, and a lot of daydreaming about Friday night's Lotaburger dinner.

Again, it was a tough hike (probably more than 15 miles on Friday alone), but we all made it. We have great memories now and a greater closeness to one another. We had a couple of awesome firesides and tons of time crammed under a tarp playing "13." Yup, what a great trip! Anyways, that Lotaburger tasted crazy good, though we probably put them out of business. All of the weight we lost that week we put back on in that one meal. (The exception is Naegle, who never lost weight. He actually gained two pounds, which kind of figures since he ate half of everyone's dinner plus his own, and he had huge lunches, which included crackers with summer sausage, peanut butter, ketchup, and topped with easy cheese. Mmmmmm...That kid has a stomach of steel!) So our trip was over, and we slept in warm beds that night...

The way I see it, backpacking is a lot like life. Life will never be easy. I don't care who you are, at some point in your life you will find yourself tired, broken down, and complaining: "Why is this happening to me?" If we keep on moving, however, never letting our focus leave our main goal, we can make it to the end. Sometimes storms hit, more times in one person's life than another. During those times, I find it really does help to stop and shelter yourself from that storm, to relax and enjoy life. Figuratively take out your cards and play "13."

The 50-mile backpacking trip we took taught me many things because I took the steps necessary to make it to the end. When our group first split up in slow and fast groups, we thought it would be easier to get ahead and carry an extra backpack for those in the slow group. However, we soon learned that this method was too tiring, and it took away from the experience of those people in the slow group. We found the most effective method of pushing our little group forward was to walk with them, encourage them, and take their mind off the difficult task that lay ahead.

In life, we may think we are traveling alone. But, in reality, there are others who have the same goals we have. How difficult would it be if you were in the slow group and yet had no encouragement from the others, no helping hand? Think of a goal in your life. How does this apply? I know that I sometimes surpass my fellow students in classes we take together. I am in the fast group, whereas some of my friends fall short into the slower group. I could leave them to fend for themselves, but what good is that going to do? I could travel faster, yet think of that poor person who is stuck in the slow group. They might throw down their pack, their walking stick, and sit down, refusing to move.

A member of a group that refuses to move can really halt the progress of that group, even when everyone else is doing all that they can to push forward. In life, this person may hold feelings of resentment and bitter hate towards those that refuse to help him. Hurt feelings and broken dreams seem to come from only serving yourself.

When we carried the others' backpacks for them, it was as though we were cheating for them. It created feelings of inferiority. If the end of the trail were, instead of making 50 miles, getting an MD, would you really want your doctor to be one of those people shuttled in the slow group?

Instead of carrying the others' backpacks, we found that encouraging and helping them had a much greater outcome. Each individual has a greater sense of self-worth, knowing that they could make the backpacking trip with enough hard work and dedication. It was also a great help to have encouraging words. I think that those who are privileged to be in the fast group have an obligation to help those that may be struggling. This does not mean we carry their pack, but maybe we just lighten the load. This is accomplished by offering to help in areas they may be struggling, or just being there with them to encourage them as they start to falter.

We may also make bad decisions and be the one slowing down our group. That was me, swimming across an icy lake, and staying in even as dark cloud rolled in and rain started to fall. Luckily, my dad was prepared with extra clothes and the knowledge of treating hypothermia. He quickly performed first aid by getting me dry and warm, and sending me to the tent in my sleeping bag once I was definitely warmed up. I would say that it is never a bad thing to over-prepare, as long as it does not weigh you down and stop your progress. By over-preparing with extra clothes, my dad probably saved my life. By over-preparing for the goals you set, you will be able to rely on your preparedness when it becomes necessary.

On a previous backpacking trip, I came over-prepared by bringing four extra dinners, which is a lot of food to carry. It wasn't a burden to my back, and I thought it would be a nice little reward for reaching my destination. However, when we got a few days in to the mountains, I soon found that there were scouts who had under-prepared and were short a few dinners. I ended up giving out my extra food with none to spare, and we were all content with the nutrition that we obtained through these meals (though I gave away one of my precious beef-stroganoff dinners, to my great disappointment).

Before starting out on a backpacking trip, it is essential to prepare. I always have a list of essentials that I will look over, making sure that I have everything packed accessibly into compartments of my backpack. Here are a few of the necessities on my list:

- Water/food/snacks
- First aid kit/whistle/fire starters
- Duct tape/pocketknife
- Sleeping bag/tent
- Map and compass/GPS

Though these are only a few items on my list, I would like to go over them and demonstrate how they are important in surviving a 50-mile backpacking trip.

Water/food/snacks: it is probably obvious that if you spend all day walking, you are going to need both nourishment and hydration. High calorie food and snacks are necessary to provide the energy needed for the constant use of your muscles backpacking requires. Water is also lost from your body, even if you don't feel like you are sweating that much. Many times, it evaporates quickly, turning you into a human swamp-cooler. Not many people realize that you also lose much water through our breathing. As oxygen needs increase, you breathe more, resulting in a greater loss of water and a greater need for hydration. Water allows all of your cells to function correctly. It also allows our body to remove wastes and toxins that build up in our bloodstream.

First aid kit/whistle/Fire starters: when you are traveling in a scarcely trekked wilderness area, accidents are prone to happen. The main use of my first aid kit has been using moleskin to prevent blister formation or rupture on the feet of many scouts with poorly fitting boots. However, it has also been used for more serious injuries, including sprained ankles, major wounds, and profuse bleeding. Being ready with the proper first aid equipment can prevent you from losing time on your journey. It can do as little as provide some comfort to as much as preventing death.

On March 21-22, 2003, I attended the annual Klondike Derby for my scouting district. On Friday afternoon, we left for the Sandia mountains to find a nice camping spot and to get some sledding in before the actual competition. This evening, one scout, a boy named Brad, went out sledding by himself (his first mistake—you should always have a buddy!) while we were setting up our tents and preparing our camp. However, I was the only one who noticed that he had left.

After about fifteen minutes, I began to worry about Brad. Anything can happen while you are in the mountains and trying to survive. So, I went out in search of him. I easily found the indention of a sled in the snow, and I followed its path for about five minutes, wondering how far Brad actually went.

Suddenly, I saw the faint outline of an orange sled, upside down and sticking out of the snow. I broke into a run, scenarios of what might have happened running through my head. I saw Brad, his overly large coat mottled with snow. He looked up at me with a dazed look in his eyes. I asked him what had happened, but Brad could not seem to remember. He was dizzy and uncoordinated, and his words seemed to slur together. Based on the location of his sled, it looked as though he had run into a large rock and fallen out of the sled, probably sustaining a moderate concussion.

Brad was scratched up quite a bit, and he had a laceration on his head, which was oozing blood. Luckily, I always carried my first aid kit on my belt, so I was able to hastily clean and cover his wounds. Since his jacket was filled with snow, I quickly got him out of it and put him in mine. He then started to shake uncontrollably, and I knew that he was probably hypothermic. I set him on the sled and promptly pulled him back to camp.

When back at camp, I was able to turn Brad's care over to my leaders. They watched him to make sure his condition didn't worsen. They got him completely out of his wet clothes and into dry ones. They sat him by the fire with hot chocolate and made sure that he recovered well.

In this example, I used my first aid kit, but it was more important that I knew the principles of first aid and scouting. I knew that it was not a smart idea for Brad to sled by himself, and I acted upon that instinct. Here is another good example of going by Murphy's Law and preparing for anything that can happen (because it probably will).

Whistles are not the first thing people think of bringing on a backpacking trip, but they are certainly essential. It is for personal safety; a whistle will signal to others if you are lost. Take the example of an older scout a few years back. While camping, he decided to make his own little camp away from everyone else. He was a great scout, so no one really thought anything of it. He took a radio with him just in case he needed anything.

While building a fire, this scout decided he needed smaller pieces of wood. He took out his hatchet and laid a piece of wood against a log. While stabilizing the log with his foot, he began to chop. After a couple of swings, the hatchet slipped and slid off the wood, right into the scout's Gore-Tex boots. It did not stop there but continued deep into his foot.

Luckily, this scout was able to do a quick butterfly stitch job on his foot, but he realized he needed more to hold the wound closed than just the stitches. He couldn't put any weight on his foot, so he radioed in to camp, but it was over a hill and not in his line of sight. Quickly he pulled out his whistle and blew three short blasts, three long blasts, three short blasts. "SOS," the international distress signal. He blew again. After just a few minutes, his troop found him and helped him back to camp. Whistles are helpful for rescue if you get lost, and even the best of us do. Yelling could work, but your voice gives out much more quickly than does a whistle.

Fire starters are also essential. Not only do they provide you with a way to stay warm and comfortable, they too can save your life. How else can you cook any food unless you have fire starters? What more effective way is there to treat hypothermia than by placing a victim near a fire and giving them hot chocolate to drink? Believe me; I've been in that situation many times.

Not only do you need a first aid kit, whistle, and fire starters, but you also need to know how to use the supplies you have. Luckily, if you buy a pre-made kit, it will usually have a user's manual in with it. But who actually reads the users manual? Who even knows such a manual exists until an emergency happens? First aid often needs to be provided quickly, and the time spent flipping through a book may be the time needed to save a life. Again, I will reiterate the motto of the Boy Scouts of

America: Be Prepared. You must always be prepared for what can happen, especially when miles away from any civilization.

Duct tape/pocketknife: these two items have been on my essentials list ever since my first backpacking trip. Thinking I was being funny, I brought the duct tape along. However, after fixing a backpack strap that tore half way during the trip using a moderate amount of duct tape, I realized that it is a necessity; it can repair, build, etc. I have used duct tape to fix backpacks, broken tent poles, leaking tents, and shoes. I have built shelters and made clotheslines. Duct tape is one of the most versatile pieces of equipment ever invented.

Pocketknives are also multi-purposed. They can be used to cut your duct tape in the configuration that you so need. They can be used to cut rope into different length pieces. They can be used as cooking and eating utensils. They can be used as pastime, carving wood or setting up throwing-knife ranges. They can be used in first aid to cut away the dead skin of a wound. Just make sure you know how to use a knife, for they can also be the cause of great destruction, including damage to equipment if not properly stored, or damage to yourself or others if not properly handled.

Sleeping bag/tent: although there are many campers who do not believe they need a sleeping bag or a tent, I assure you that there are times when you will want them. They are necessary both for comfort and for safety, such as with hypothermia (and no, you usually don't need to be naked in the bag or have another person with you; sorry to ruin your dreams). I have experienced many wilderness survival nights without these two essentials. On a few of the occasions, I was fine. It was warm, and I have trained myself to sleep in almost any condition. Almost.

My very first survival campout took place when I was twelve. We were allowed only a garbage bag and a pocketknife to take with us, and we were required to build a shelter and sleep out one night in the middle of nowhere. "This should be exciting!" I thought to myself. So, I got on with the building of my shelter. Being young and inexperienced, I really didn't understand weather patterns, strategy in the placement and design of a shelter, etc. I was proud of my shelter when I finished—it rather looked like a little boat dug into the ground with branches randomly covering it and the garbage bag sprawled across the top. Then the storm rolled in.

It started to hail, which is probably better than rain because it didn't soak my clothes. However, tiny hail balls covered the ground and started to melt. Water started to flow downhill, heading for the exact location of my little shelter. I did not know what to do. It was late, and I was tired from a day full of activities.

I grabbed the garbage bag from the top of my shelter and wrapped it tightly around me. I laid awake all night, shivering, my back soaked from lying in a puddle of icy water. At 5:00 am, my leader said he would come and get all of the scouts. Instead, I went to find him. I felt that I needed to get warm or I would die. I completed the campout, but I did not sleep for more than five minutes. Immediately after, I tiredly stumbled to my tent, stripped off all of my wet clothes, and crawled into my sleeping bag. I fell fast asleep until the early afternoon.

Many people might think that it is all right to go a couple of nights without sleeping, especially when you are in the wilderness. The truth is that when you are backpacking or trying to survive, sleep is more essential then ever. Without sleep, you won't be able to think straight or get much accomplished. Without a tent and sleeping bag, you probably won't be getting the necessary amount of sleep.

Map and compass/GPS: the last thing on my list is a map and navigating device, though it certainly is not the least important. When planning a backpacking trip, you must first obtain a topographical map of the location you wish to visit. Of course, you also need to learn how to read a topographical map, including the symbols and topographical (elevation) markings. After learning how to read the map, you then look at your options for a trip, taking into account your skill level and difficulty of the terrain.

You first find a starting point, a nice place where you can bring your car up and begin your hike. Then you find where you want to end—if it is somewhere other than the beginning, you will need someone to move your vehicle for you. After these two locations have been picked, you then find trails to hike that will lead from the beginning to the end. You can use the elevation markings to estimate how difficult the hike will be—how many feet elevation change is there in a certain distance? Many trails lead to the same destination, so it may take some time to find one that really fits your needs, whether you are just beginning or are an experienced outdoorsman.

After planning your trail and marking it on the map, it is nice to jot down approximate distances of trails before forks, etc. It may also be helpful to mark waypoints into a GPS or calculate bearings for a compass. If you are using a compass, it may be nice to know how far average you travel in a certain amount of time so that you can calculate the distance you have traveled. As a general rule of thumb, the more work you put in preparing for the trip, the easier the trip will be along the way. The more you study and learn the map, the less likely you will be in getting lost, and the more likely you will be in getting yourself out of a bad situation.

On the recent 50-mile backpacking trip that we went on, it would have been impossible to get to our destination had we not carefully planned the trail and plot waypoints into a GPS. Due to recent fires in the mountains where we were hiking, the trails were completely obliterated. Many of us searched for trails, but eventually we realized that we were wasting too much time and not getting anywhere. We learned to rely on the GPS to guide us to the waypoints we set before our trip even began.

In an earlier 35-mile backpacking trip, we had a similar problem. When traversing areas that are scarcely in use, trails are not as distinct as they usually would be. Often, we would lose our way; somehow, we always seemed to end up on the wrong trail. Our GPS systems would confirm this and show where we were. However, as younger scouts, we also wanted to learn to find our position just by using a map and a compass. We learned the process of *triangulation*, or using discreet peaks in the distance, matching the up with the map, and finding our precise location. Both the GPS and triangulation confirmed our location, and we were able to find how to get back on the correct trail.

NINE

WHY does backpacking remind me of life? To begin with, we need a map, and we need some sort of system of navigation. Everyone is in a different stage of his or her life, so each individual needs his or her own map. A school age child's map may start at his life at the present moment, but his destination or goal might be to make more friends. Now the question is which trail he will take. Does he think he will make more friends if he becomes a bully? Or is it better to share his toys and play with other kids?

As we get older, we get increasingly more maps, big and small, and more decisions to make on which trails to take. The trails become more difficult. Starting in high school, I have had many maps to look at before me. One of my goals was to make the best grades possible. Even for this seemingly simple goal, I can get lost on many paths. The trail I chose to take was to do my own work, finish my homework, and study for tests. Though this may look like an easy path, there are easier, and as I saw them, I would occasionally drift away from the one I had chosen.

Take cheating, for example. In high school, it is commonplace to see homework being copied and questions on an upcoming test being passed around. What an easy path to my goal! I can copy this student's paper and look up answers to test questions in advance! But I have to ask myself, "What is the purpose of my trip?" Sure, I go backpacking to have a good time. However, if that was the only reason, I could have just stayed home and played games. I go for the challenge, for the experience, for the knowledge and wisdom I gain on the way.

When I get good grades, I know that the work I put in is getting me a nice scholarship for college. But is that my only incentive? If it is, I might as well be cheating my way through. I want the experience and the knowledge that I can actually do it. If I get good grades just for money, it is likely that I won't do my best once I get to a post-secondary school, and I am prone to blow any academic scholarship. However, if I am dedicated and do my best, yet do not get that money reward, it is likely that I can go to college, continue to work hard and excel, leading to scholarships after my first semester.

Another map I may have in high school is the map to having friends and building strong relationships. As you can imagine, this can be accomplished in countless ways, many of which are equally acceptable. It all depends on who you are and what end result you are hoping for.

With each situation in your life, you can probably think of the goal you are trying to reach and where you are starting. Just as it is vitally important to study out your map before starting on a backpacking trip, it is important to evaluate your situation and decide what is best for you based on your current physical, mental, emotional, and moral standings.

Oftentimes when backpacking, you find that the trail you set out on was too difficult or not challenging enough. When this is the case, you pull out your map and decide if it is worth making it to that goal. If it is, you can start working on a different trail, though it is often difficult to find and reach. If you do not find that goal necessary, you can turn back and start your journey with another map in a different location.

If a goal is important, and yet you can't seem to reach it, or you get lost on the way, there are navigation systems available. With the world ever changing, new technology and information are becoming easily accessible. If you have the luxury of owning a GPS, maybe by having easy access to the Internet, then the flow of information is at your fingertips, and you can research different ways to reach your goals. You may hire tutors; you may start independent study courses or classes at a community college to further your education.

If you only own your compass and your map, it will take more time to find where you're at and try to locate a different route. You need to take the time to triangulate, finding objects in the distance that can aid in answering your questions. This help may come through another individual such as a friend, associate, or professional. It may mean traveling down to a public library and doing your own research.

No matter what your situation, there is always a way out, whether easy or hard. And though life may be much more difficult if you are born into an underprivileged family, I sincerely believe that the effort you take to change your life will only be for your good.

The other supplies on my essentials list are those things you use while on your journey. Starting with food, water, sleeping bags, tents, all of which are self-explanatory—you need to take care of your physical health and emotional health. I believe that moderation in all things is the way to bring balance into your life. No matter what trail you're choosing to pursue, it is most important to take care of yourself, even above reaching that goal. I mean, what would be the point of pursuing a profession, accomplishing something great, if you killed yourself before you reached the end?

I know many people who have the same goal as me—get the best grades possible. While preparing for their journey, all too many of them forgot to take along with them adequate food, water, and sleeping bags. More than once a week, I hear of friends who stay up until all hours of the night studying for a test. Then, trying to get all the sleep they can (which is usually only a couple of hours), they skip breakfast, probably the most important brain-food meal of the day. Using my philosophy, I put myself first, and though I will still study, I will not obsess over it and compromise my mental state. What is the point of studying if you are too tired or too hungry to easily recall that which you have studied?

I also know people who will take too many sleeping bags with them, too heavy a tent, sacrificing room for food and water, but also weighing them down, lowering their rate of productivity. What is the point? I have seen no benefits to sleeping longer than eight hours. In fact, I feel better rested when I sleep seven hours than when I sleep twelve. Why is that? I really don't know, but it is as though we force our bodies to lose all drive to do anything productive.

When we eat too little because of being "too busy," or we eat too much because of being "too stressed," we also put ourselves at risk for many other problems. When we force ourselves to cope with excess stress (which includes abnormal amounts of food and sleep), our bodies have to use energy to try to maintain homeostasis. This compromises our immune system and makes us susceptible to infection and injury. Our habits now will also affect us in the future. Bad diet and sleep patterns will carry on and put us at risk for multiple diseases and disorders.

As you make your way on the journey of life, you should also have the following items: a first aid kit, a whistle, fire starters, duct tape, and a pocketknife. What do these items all have in common? They can all get you out of trouble, but only if you are willing to bring them along on your trip. In our real-life example, this tool is known as education.

Just as a first aid kit can make your journey more comfortable or even prevent death so that you can reach your destination, so can education make the trail to your goal possible, even enjoyable, to pursue. Just as the scout used his whistle to call for help, your education can be a call to employers to hire you and improve your situation. Just as fires can help save you and comfort you, an education can save you from debt and help you know that everything will be okay. Just as duct tape and pocketknives are versatile tools that can repair, build, and create, education can build a new future and create opportunities for you to excel in your pursuits. Education is the key that unlocks the gate of opportunity.

The skills I learned while backpacking also help when I am not hitting the trails hard. Life is similar, for what we learn while pursuing something difficult can benefit us in other aspects of our lives. The people skills learned while working as a cashier can benefit us while trying to interview for a different job. The nursing skills I have been learning have not only helped with my medical abilities, but I am more compassionate, aware of other people's feelings, and able to "read" non-verbal communication for cues of what to say.

The first aid I learned through backpacking and Boy Scouts has helped whenever I see someone who is injured, no matter how big or small the wound may be. Just recently, I was in the kitchen helping my mom make dinner. I was slicing potatoes with a large, extremely sharp knife, so my mom told me, "You really need to be careful. Make sure you curl your fingers in so you don't cut them off!"

I listened to her warning, and after I cut, she placed the potatoes in a pan. She started to fry them and wanted some butter in the pan, so she took out a butter knife and a stick of butter. She made the mistake of holding the butter with her left hand as she cut down with her right hand. The butter was being cut slowly at first, so she applied more pressure, and as she did so, the knife slipped quickly through the butter and into her finger.

I heard my mom let out a cry as she ran past me, saying that she had cut her finger. Seeing as she was holding a butter knife, I didn't think it would be too bad. However, when I saw a deep gash that went almost to the bone, I knew that she needed quick first aid. She really needed stitches, but I knew that super glue would work just as well. As my dad got his first aid kit, I showed my mom how to put pressure on her finger and raise it above her heart as I covered it with a paper towel. When my dad returned, we found that we didn't have super glue, so instead we used butterfly stitches and Band-Aids.

However, my mom's finger did not stop bleeding, partly due to the awkward location of the cut. So, my dad drove to Wal-Mart as I consoled my mom, who repeatedly whispered, "But it was just a butter knife..."—she was in shock because of what had happened, so I had to continually reassure her that everything was going to be all right. When my dad returned, the cut was still bleeding profusely. My dad held my mom's wound closed as I applied super glue. Within a few seconds, the bleeding had stopped, and my mom was fine.

Because I was prepared with the knowledge of how to care for a wound and treat for different types of shock, I was able to help my mom and make the experience as least traumatic as possible, both physically and emotionally. Just as years of scouting has prepared me for situations like this, the more we work on the journey of life, the better prepared we can be to face the challenges and situations of every day living. We can stand up for what we believe in and make a difference in the world.

7-16-06

...Onto the backpacking! It was pretty fun, but not long enough. On Friday morning, we left for the mountain [Wheeler Peak, the highest peak in New Mexico], a fairly long drive up past Taos. The hike started up hill and continued so about the entire way. I was fine doing it, but some of the younger scouts (Dillon and Landon, *cough cough*) were having a difficult time. To speed them up and slow me down, I carried two

backpacks most of the way. We started switching off so Jacob took it for quite a while and Naegle took it for a bit.

By the end of the first day, we were pooped. We set up camp in a nice little location, drank hot Crystal Light, played cards, and wrestled. We crashed that night after a great fireside and woke up the next morning for another day of hiking.

Just yesterday, we left our backpacks at camp and hiked into Wheeler Peak. Landon and Brother Barnett turned back before arriving (again, it was all up hill), but the rest of us made it. We spent some time trying to signal another scout troop on top of Sandia Peak with signal mirrors until the sun was covered with clouds. We peed off the highest point in New Mexico, hand-fed marmots, and signed our names in a little booklet at the top of the peak. Cool. All of this on my 17th birthday.

What was most fun was yet to come. There had been a helicopter crash in just the past week up at Horseshoe Lake just below Wheeler. We decided to off-road it and go straight down. Dillon and Naegle thought this was a bad idea, seeing how we would have to head straight back up to get out, so they turned back and headed towards camp. So, Jacob, my dad, and I headed to the helicopter crash and took some pictures. That was neat, even though we weren't allowed to get close enough to touch it. A ranger named Eddy made sure of that, although he did tell us what had happened and watched us swim in Horseshoe Lake. That's what we did next.

We went down to the lake, stripped down to our boxers, and got in the lake, a difficult task only because the water was literally freezing. Above us, there was still snow melting off and filling the lake. We finally swam a few laps and took some pictures. Getting out, drying off, and hiking on was refreshing after our little swim. However, getting to the top of the mountain was even more difficult than it had originally appeared.

Jacob had sprained his ankle coming down, but somehow he made it out of the canyon and continued hiking ten miles on it without too much trouble. Getting out of the canyon killed me. It was like climbing a couple thousand feet in a couple hundred yards, maybe worse. So, when we came back to camp we were dead. We packed up and headed out. The good thing is that it was almost all down hill to get out.

I was in the fast group, and we were done about an hour before everyone else. We played "13" and waited. Since we have so much time to talk while backpacking, I know that Landon likes J.C., Dillon likes Courtney and a girl from Australia named Rachel, and Naegle likes Courtney. They all know that I like all members of the opposite sex, within limits.

I love backpacking. I mean, us guys bonding—you can't experience anything like that except for up in the mountains. When we got out, we went to Dairy Queen and headed on home. We watched a movie in the car (as we did on the way up), and I played some Sudoku on my Nintendo Dual Screen. We got home around 8:30 pm, so by the time I cleaned up (mostly) and showered and stuff, I went to bed. In these two days, I lost six pounds, though it's probably all water weight. My oldest brother got me a cool PS-2 game for my birthday. Man! All of these games I want to play, but at the same time I don't want to be unproductive! Talk about a love-hate relationship...

TEN

So school started. Yay. If you couldn't tell, I was being sarcastic. I missed a bunch, but I'll try to fill you in quickly 'cause I gotta get to bed. I haven't been keeping up with my journaling only because of a crazy load of homework almost every night. On top of that, there are dates, parties to crash, and lifting weights. So let me fill you in.

I don't like school. I don't like nursing. But, I really want to finish out this year strong and do my absolute best. In English, we've already had like five tests, and we've only been in school seven days. AP Biology, probably the hardest class offered at La Cueva, is just that—hard. However, I love classes like it so I think I'm gonna have an amazing time as well as learn a ton. We started clinicals in nursing already. It is Thursday, Friday, and every other Wednesday. This week, I started work at the VA hospital, and boy do I loathe it! There are no supplies, all of the patients are crazy old guys, and there's absolutely no communication, no paper work, etc. Aaah! Get me out of there! On Friday of this week, I had a patient who, after I gave him a bed bath and changed his linens and everything, stated calmly, "I think I had an accident." This was at the very end of my shift, before reporting off and running back to school. But there I was, stuck doing the dirty work. BM everywhere, a smell that can make the strongest of us lose our cool and vomit. Luckily, I didn't lose control, but I came close.

So let me tell you about my crazy awesome social life. On Saturday, I decided to crash the West stake dance with a bunch of people from my ward. It was me, Lani and Rachel, Naegle, and Baby D. Us guys all wore jeans, pink button up shirts, and a white undershirt. Low and behold, we were kicked out of the dance because we were wearing jeans. So, we drove all the way back to our houses and changed into black pants while the girls threw on skirts. We finally got to the dance, and that's just what we did. I slow danced, swinged, break-danced, did a little salsa, line danced, etc. Almost my entire squad from youth conference was there, the exception being Jenessa.

71

So I boogied with Amanda, Annie, Smoochie, etc. Really fun, but we got home late and I was dead for church the next day.

Then it was this first full week of school. I found that after nursing, if I speed like a mad man, I can stop by my house before going to seminary and make it on time. So, that's what I've been doing. The bad thing is that I'm never informed about what's going on at La Cueva, so I always show up way early whenever there is an assembly. Oh well, better early than late, I guess.

So yeah, nursing is fun, not including the boring lectures and clinicals (98% of it). English is okay, but we have tons of crazy tests, my teacher is pretty crazy, and there's lots of homework. AP Biology is crazy awesome without exception. I love the class content, the teacher, the labs, and everything. This may soon change, but at the moment, I love it.

Two Wednesdays ago, we had a pool party for a young men/young women activity. The day after our Zoolander party (which included swimming, lots of crazy diving board flips, and a movie with a big group), we went to Sandia pool for swimming with the Cherry Hills youth. We ended up going with the Hardys whom we invited. The Schmutz's were there, as well as Amanda. So all we did was crazy stuff off the diving boards like at the Zoolander party. This time, I did a belly flop, back flop, and unintentional side flop off the high dive. Needless to say, I was quite red and bruised afterwards. It was fun. I ended up getting Amanda's email address, so we're keeping in touch.

Last Friday after school, Naegle and I got together at my house. Everyone in my family (except for me) left to Idaho on Thursday. So, I had the house to myself. Naegle and I shared workout secrets. We started with my wrestling leg workout and concluded with Naegle's rock-climbing abs-workout. This means we did weighted squats, weighted lunges, lunges, reverse lunges, squats, jump squats, wall-sits, V-sits, scissor kicks, sit-ups, crunches, and the like. Right now, it is Sunday afternoon, and I am still aching and limping from the workout, but it was worth it.

After working out, I went on a date with Courtney (she asked me out last Sunday), and her friend Emily took out Kyle. We were gonna go to Putt-Putt Golf, but it was raining like crazy so we went bowling instead. We then watched some of Elf at *my house and departed. On Saturday, Naegle and I got together with Christa and Amanda to watch <u>Nacho Libre</u> (stupid but funny). We went out for Frostys at Wendy's then went to the dance. I tried to teach a bunch of freshman how to break dance, danced like crazy, and had a blast. Oh well, out of room. Two dates this week, I'll fill you in later!*

Life has its ups and downs. In the journal entry before this, you can probably tell that I wasn't in the best of moods. I was tired, sick of school, and just wanted things to be over. It was a storm in my life. What did I do about it? I pulled over to the side of the trail, took out my tarp, and played "13." My friends were my relief. Just being with them and taking my mind off school was a refresher.

Attitude plays a large role in life. Think back on an experience when someone you know (this may even have been yourself) had a bad attitude. What did it do to those around this person? While working in a small group for nursing my junior year of high school, a certain girl in my class had a bad attitude. Whether she was going through some hormonal changes or just having a crummy day, I could not tell, but she could not be positive about anything we were doing. Her complaining was incessant and annoying. She tried to contradict everything that anyone would say. Soon enough, everyone had the same attitude as she had.

That was my worst small-group experience. Can you imagine me, the only boy in my group, surrounded by seven moody teenage girls? Yeah, it was that bad. We got nothing done, and I ended up taking home a lot of work to finish up. Following this incidence, I could not help but get in a bad mood whenever I saw this girl. I had to learn to avoid her and not open my mouth if I didn't have anything nice to say.

There are times in my life when I get moody. It most often occurs after a difficult day, such as when I get out late from clinicals in the hospital. However, there are times when I just feel down for no apparent reason. Oftentimes, I spread my bad mood by opening my mouth and intentionally insulting others or their ideas. I don't seem to think straight during those times.

I have learned that attitude is important in pretty much anything you do. Even if you are feeling down, you don't have to let it show. I did an experiment on one of the days that I wasn't feeling too hot. I was being pretty rude to my mom, and I noticed that she immediately got in a bad mood. We really couldn't talk without starting to argue, so I stopped talking altogether.

That same day, I went to one of my classes at school where participation is necessary. I really didn't feel like talking, and I felt that I would just ruin the lesson. However, I decided to pretend as though I felt good, that nothing was wrong. So, that is what I did. The interesting thing is this: the way I acted was the way I started to feel. Because I started to be more outgoing and open, complimenting others and being myself, I found that by the end of the class, I felt great.

I went home that day to find my mom in the same kind of mood as I had left her, so I continued with my little experiment. I swallowed my pride and apologized for how I had acted. I then acted myself. I soon saw my mother's spirits lifted as I acted as though nothing had happened before this.

We can be an influence in the lives of our friends and associates just by having a good attitude. I know that the friends that I associate with always help me in this aspect. They are usually the ones helping me to not feel so down. They always ask how I am and what they can do for me. Adding to that, they follow up on their questions. They are interested in what I have to say and how I feel. If the entire world would just ask these two questions and follow up on them, how great would life be? How are you? What can I do for you? It is so simple, yet difficult to implement.

Friends have always been important in my life. When I was younger, I didn't have the support system that I do right now. I often felt alone, even though I had a little group of friends that I played with at recess. They all lived close together, within the same neighborhood, whereas I live a couple of miles away. This led to them growing closer and me being pushed further and further out of the group. Maybe this is the reason why I started doing badly in school. Maybe this is the reason why I never wanted to do anything but watch cartoons.

Friends often shape the ways our lives turn out. My middle school friends were a little immature and still obsessed with games and television. They were egocentric. One summer, I had one of my friends over almost every day. That must have been the least productive I have ever been in my life, yet I could not seem to break the pattern. We would play on our Gameboys for hours on end. Sometimes, we would go outside and build miniature villages of bugs. He was a great kid and fun to be with, but he probably wasn't the kind of friend I needed to break my trend of laziness.

The summer after I wasted my life away, I went to a Boy Scout camp at Elephant Butte. I was one of the youngest scouts there, and I often felt isolated and lonely, not being in contact with whom I considered my *best friends*. However, by spending a week with some of the boys who were only a year older than I was, I realized the level of my immaturity, and I found new examples of how I could lead my life. Those individuals became my role models. Now, had they turned me away and not allowed me to participate in the "older" activities, I would have shrunk back into my little box and would have remained immature. However, I did not, and after scout camp ended, I started working on myself, trying to be accepted by the others.

I was invited to fun activities by the older kids. I sang with them. I made movies with them. However, I soon found that I was not being myself. I would do stupid things to try to impress my peers, only to find them look down on my behavior. Luckily, I was able to see that my behavior had gone too far, and I was able to take out my compass and triangulate, trying to find where I was at and how I could get back to my goal.

My goal happened to be to make friends, and I found I was doing this in the wrong way. I was going on a path that seemed exciting and foreign, but it really would end in ruining my identity. I looked at my situation, and I decided to change my destination. "Yes, friends are important, but so is my future. I want to be the best person possible, following what I know is right." With my new way of life, I found something incredible happened—friends started coming to me.

Before I was trying to find where I fit in. After, I started becoming who I wanted to be, not letting peer influence alter my actions. When I did this, I made friends because I became more outgoing and compassionate. I tried to be everyone's friend, and by doing so, I found others who were trying to be their best.

As my actions continued in the course I set out, I found my friends had similar qualities to me, meaning that while I tried to do my best, they knew what I was going through and encouraging me. I guess you could say that this is how you find your backpacking group. Those on the same trail as yourself know how difficult it is and know what helps them through. With this knowledge, they can help you when you start slowing down or feeling discouraged, or you can help them. It turns into a circle of trust and sincere care and affection. True friends are amazing. That's just the way it is.

ELEVEN

...*ALLEN* and I always sit outside for lunch with our group of Mormons. All too conspicuously, Courtney and Andrea talked to each other about how no one asked them to homecoming, how people thought they were going out with Dallin and Brandon respectively, and how they wanted to get together that night and watch chick-flicks. It was way too obvious to over look, so Allen and I planned how we were going to ask them.

After seminary one day, we left in my car and went to Smith's to buy a bouquet of roses each. We randomly sat down at lunch with our roses and acted as if nothing were different as we ate. We waited until the very end of lunch until someone asked what we were up to, and then we turned to our dates and asked them if they would not go to homecoming with us. I asked Andrea and Allen asked Courtney. We then told them that they were to wear formals and we would pick them up at 6:00 pm on Saturday. So, we had to plan. I had a good idea from Jacob's birthday party—we had gone to a place called Itz and had a blast. The Hardys came as well as Naegle and some family. There was a crazy awesome little bowling alley, some rides, tons of games, and more. I told Allen about this and we planned to go.

Saturday came, and Allen and I got together. I was wearing a nice suit with a light blue shirt and dark blue tie, all new that I bought that day. We picked up our dates and didn't even tell them where we were going. When we pulled up into the Hooter's parking lot, we all got a good laugh. We went into Itz, which is really close to Hooter's, and paid for admission plus games on a card. When the total came out to over $80, I looked at Allen and we paid for fewer games, bringing the total to about $60. I paid $20 and Allen paid the rest.

We had dinner in the movie room where we watched <u>Grease</u> for a bit, and then we went and played games. Bowling came first, where we used most of our points.

It was funny because Naegle was also there, so we said hi, all dressed up in our formals. Then we played some Mario Kart, shopped around, and left for the movie theaters. We went to Century 24 where Allen got us in for free to watch The Guardian, *a very good and intense movie about the coast guard. We then went our separate ways after an awesome evening. I kind of feel bad since Allen basically paid for everything (plus it was his first real date). In addition, Andrea bought me a boutonnière and I didn't get her a corsage. She said it was fine since I had bought her all of those roses, but still, I felt bad. At least it was fun.*

Oh well, school, nursing, wrestling, Pre-med club—they are all taking over my life. At least I'm having fun, and it's what I want to do. Tomorrow is a day off school for fall break, which should be really nice in order to catch up on homework and have fun. I have been doing homework and watching movies all weekend—maybe I should do something physical. I just can't wait until this school year is over. I will finally get to work for money, leave for college, and do what I want to do.

I have been getting slightly down lately thinking, "Why am I doing this?" I have contemplated dropping out right now and just going to college, but I really want to finish what I am working at. I cannot drop out! I am actually going to apply to BYU this November, so it's really exciting. Plus the fact that I'm almost half done with my senior year! Yay! Well, life goes on. I wrote a great application essay** into BYU, so hopefully I can get a good scholarship. Well, there's nothing really else to write. To tell you the truth, I love my life. I don't think I would change anything, even if I had the choice.

**10-5-06

He was a newborn, only a few hours old. Gripping his tiny leg in one hand and a 23-gauge needle and syringe in the other, I felt a drop of sweat fall from under my light-blue scrubs. An overzealous grandmother watched over my shoulder and videotaped her new little grandson being held in my shaking hands. The needle came down quickly and hit the newborn's thigh. The feeling of human skin breaking is much different from a model or an orange. I cringed at first, expecting the infant to kick or scream. He didn't. It was a miracle.

As a student nurse, some of my friends laugh at me. Whenever they sarcastically say "Male nurse!" blood rushes to my face. They probably don't realize what I have been through. Their laughter has only served to strengthen my character, and though I still get chagrined at times, I know that if I can handle the stress of putting in suppositories, giving shots, and changing older people's diapers (believe me, it's much more pleasant with infants), then I can handle anything.

Last year, my schedule began at 5:45 am and clinical rotations at the hospital often lasted until 7:00 pm. I had to give up a year of wrestling, orchestra, and my shot at being valedictorian in order to do this. My sacrifices were well worth it, however, because of the knowledge and experience I gained. As a senior in high school, I have learned to handle nursing, two AP classes, seminary, Pre-med club, wrestling, Boy Scouts, church and youth activities, and more. This sets me apart from other applicants—a willingness and ability to learn in order to serve my fellow man.

Nursing had started to take over my life. You can probably see that the hospital has become a major theme in much of my writing, probably because it is the place where I have the most experience. After two years of working in the hospital setting, I guess you could say that I was starting to get the hang of it.

1-27-07

In nursing, I am working at the specialties hospital for clinicals. Last week, I went to Highland High School and worked with a program they have for physically and mentally disabled teenagers and young adults. My day in the hospital was interesting— I had a depressing patient. She had a progressing Guillain-Barré Syndrome. It completely paralyzed her body, except her head and neck, and it paralyzed her diaphragm, forcing her to have a tracheotomy attached to a ventilator to survive. I did tracheotomy care, lots of suctioning, etc. It was pretty neat. But, I was assigned a crap load of homework, which is what I did last Friday and Saturday.

This week, I took care of a lady with a history of a crud load of respiratory infections. She was elderly and hospitalized with respiratory failure. Because of this, she was intubated and ventilated. Because she could no longer eat, she had a percutaneous endoscopic gastrostomy (PEG) tube in place for enteral feedings. On top of this, she had a copious amount of nasty sputum that tended to clog her ventilator tubes about once an hour (even with occasional suctioning). This sputum was frothy and tan in color (at first I thought it was her tube-feeding formula) and smelled like death. Agg, I'm gagging right now just thinking about it! It was also MRSA positive, so whenever I was in the room I had to be gowned and gloved.

But wait! There's more! She had very weak pelvic floor muscles, and since she had so much sputum built up, she would constantly cough (from her trach), causing an increase in intra-abdominal pressure and forcing her uterus outside of her body. It was pretty gross because this happened almost every hour, her prolapsing uterus (if you don't know what that is or looks like, I am happy for you). This wasn't the worst part, oh no. This is it (try not to be too grossed out): I put it back in. Yup, kind of weird, holding a lady's uterus in my hand and literally shoving it back in her body until feeling it pop into place. It was worth it just for the story and the experience. How many 17 year olds can say they have replaced a prolapsed uterus? How exciting.

On Thursday, I also experienced some interesting stuff. I went around with the wound nurse and had a great time. I saw a nasty foot wound on this guy's heel, open enough that you could see the bone. I was able to clean it and dress it, etc. Cool. What was even cooler, though, was the next wound I saw.

It was on this crazy old lady's back. (Side note—she was crazy, yet she called me crazy and told me to "shut up" when I wasn't talking. She also told me she was going to hit me. An angry, crazy old lady...). The wound was on her sacral area and was huge—bigger than those I had even seen in my book! It was about 10-12 cm in diameter and about 5-6 cm in depth, which was smaller than when she had originally come in. Half of my hand fit in it, and there was tunneling so I could reach down further into the wound cavity. It was so deep that I could feel and see her spine. This wound was a decubitus ulcer (bed sore). Amazing, huh?

Even cooler was that the wound nurse gave me charge over the entire care for this large wound. That meant that I went in with equipment and scraped out the dead tissue, used a high pressure cleaner to irrigate the wound, dried it, stuffed it with hyperosmolar gauze, and put a dressing on it, taping it to her back. It was, again, incredible. So, these were my amazing experiences. Cool, eh?

...In English, we went over Dante's Inferno *recently. We were tested over it and assigned to create our own Hell. Mine is pretty much amazing, so I'm putting it in here*** for your enjoyment. I wrote it in* terza rima, *or third rhyme, which was invented by Dante. I had better get a good grade because I worked on this for an entire week! You can really get a sense of a person by how he writes. See if you can pick up the subtle, dark humor and amazing writing techniques used. (Just kidding...)...*

***1-14-07

The Hospital's Hell

My work on night shift was going too
slow,
Heavy eyes closed, drool dripping from
my mouth,
When a voice said, "Wake up. Look
down below.

I'm a spirit from Hell here to lead you,
And guide you through this, life's
denouement
With the retribution that will ensue."

Circle 1

"Where am I?" I gasped, a horrified cry.
The air was dark, the walls endless
and gray.
A loud, ringing noise answered in reply.

A man ran past at magnificent speed,
Answering call-lights, then
answering more—
Angry old men screaming, "Hurry!"
"Indeed,"

Said the spirit, "He pays for his offense,

This Pestering Patient cared not for
his nurse,
Incessantly asking for favors immense.

His punishment is eternally this:
Now he's the nurse with infinite
patients
Who never stop talking and never
dismiss."

Circle 2

I walked down the hallway fearing what
I saw,
But never prepared for what I found
next.
The yelling, the screaming, it made me
withdraw.

"Come, watch," the spirit quietly
beckoned,
"These are the Pompous Personnel
who lived
To hassle young students at every
second.

Now in their death, knowledge is taken,
Forever harassed by intelligent
men."
Tears filled my eyes when I saw those
forsaken,

Devoid of all knowledge, hope, and
reason.
I continued my long journey through
Hell
Fearing for the future, sins, and treason.

Circle 3

The smell battered my nose before I saw
A group of staff covered in
excrement,
And what they were doing made me drop
jaw.

They rolled the old men who lay on bed
rest,
And changed the bedpans that rest
underneath.
Lying back down, those men put to the
test

The poor group of staff that smelled of
BM.
For the aged men could not hold in
their stool.
The staff changed each bedpan again and
again.

Suddenly I saw Bill from morning shift
And asked him what happened, why
he was here.
"I never did my job, I would just drift

Day after day, making aides do my work.
Ever I'm forced to change bedpans
because
I assigned it to others—now I'm
berserk!"

We said our goodbyes and I thought in
my head,
"Bill deserved this fate and fittingly
so.
I hope not to join him, for then I'd be
dead!"

Circle 4

The next round of Hell was worse than
                before.
        Poor Mr. Johnson! Poor Chris and
                poor Jill!
But what was their crime? I had to
                implore.

Mr. Johnson was a patient without hope,
        In the hospital with an abscess from
Shooting up on heroin, taking dope.

But Chris and Jill both worked with me
                for years.
        Now they were here, crawling
                through an abyss
Full of hypodermic needles, they shed
                tears,

And unable to speak, for without stop
        Their stomachs turned, forcing them
                to throw up
Slugs, each hitting the ground with a
                "Plop."

"What was their crime and what could
                they have done,
        To consign their souls forever in
                Hell,

To never feel joy, to never see sun?"

The spirit answered, an ominous voice,
        "Under lock and key lies a poison
                snake
Whose venom makes demons and devils
                rejoice.

These are the Detestable Druggies who,
        Working often with dangerous
                toxins
Gave into temptation all the way
                through.

This poison's called Morphine and
                Demerol
        And Vicodin—the list goes on and
                on.
They could no longer live on alcohol,

So they turned to a means used on the
                street.

        Though narcotics helped to dull their
                great pain,
Forever they'll suffer for their deceit."

Circle 5

Blood oozed on the floor in rivers of
pain,
Anguish of sinners who dwelled in
this round,
Droplets of blood fell in torrents of rain.

Lying on surgical tables are men
With no anesthesia, screaming in
woe.
Scalpels pierce their flesh time and time
again.

"Spirit!" I cried. "Tell me, what was their
sin?"
"Unwilling to admit making
mistakes,
They misdiagnosed and caused to begin

Unneeded surgeries, treatments, and
harm.
They entered wrong sides, causing
much anguish.
These Inept Interns caused undue alarm.

Now they're condemned to suffer
evermore,
Feeling every surgical procedure

They put their patients through, from
stitch to gore."

I walked on, happy to descry the truth,
For the doctors who once worked at
Lacelove
Would reside in this place, forever
uncouth.

Circle 6

The next round of victims were just like
before,
But the screaming was louder, the
torture
More intense, their misery cried like a
roar.

The air was thick, a smell of burning
flesh,
More blood splashed from the tables
than before.
"Hear their screams, their bodies twist
and thresh!"

The spirit seemed to smile in contempt.
Pointing towards the sinners, it
coldly said,
"These Fraudulent Physicians made the
attempt

To change patient records, cover up
                    fraud.
          In this they did succeed, but not in
                    death,
For sins are revealed, forever abroad.

Corruption is punished with corruptions,
          Forced to endure foulness of every
                    sense.
You have yet witnessed anguish
                    eruptions,

The stench of human soft tissue burning,
          The piercing sounds of slicing and
                    tearing
Of flesh. They feel nothing but a
                    yearning

For a chance to change their ways, but in
                    vain.
          They'll ceaselessly see nothing but
                    darkness,
Despair is their everlasting domain."

Circle 7

Above the door to the obstetrics room,
          Abandon hope, all ye who enter
                    here.
A sign, a warning, an impending doom.

Before the door opened, the shrieks of
                    death
          Leaked from the room like water
                    through a sieve,
Women in labor, a last dying breath.

The door opened, and that is what it was:
          Women in labor, but more than just
                    that—
Shattering echoes of wretchedness
                    because

No infants were born, but imps in their
                    place,
          Spawns of Satan whose horns ripped
                    the cervix,
Whose evil forever is shunned by God's
                    grace.

"These are the women," the spirit told
                    me,
          "The ones who destroyed many a
                    marriage—
Nurses who slept with doctors for
                    money.

They are the Treacherous Trollops
                    indeed.

Carnal desires have no place in
           Hell,
Endlessly suffering travail for greed."

I watched the devils, newly from the
           womb,
     Head to a new door, the next round
           of here.
Following lead, I entered the next room.

Circle 8

No crying I heard, a new sound for Hell,
     For I only heard malicious laughing,
No yelling, no screaming, no dreadful
           smell.

"Where are the sinners?" I marveled in
           awe.
     "Watch the newborn imps,"
                answered the spirit.
I followed them onward, seeing no flaw.

A man appeared, a blank look on his
           face,
     And the devil approached the poor
           body;
He ripped it open and entered the space.

Now as a person, he opened his palm,
     Revealing a cockroach, squirming
           and mad,
But helpless with the imp, who remained
           calm.

Laughing he tore the cockroach limb
           from limb,
     Popping its shell, squeezing out the
           entrails.
Yet the cockroach still squirmed, its life
           ne'er dim.

"This cockroach," declared the spirit,
           "contains
     The shade of the man in whose body
           now lives
The devilish imp, where he forever
           remains.

These Frequent Fliers, sick most of the
           year,
     Refused treatments to help them get
           better,
Self-medicating with chocolate and beer.

Since each refuses care for his person,
     He no longer enjoys the pleasure it
           brings.
Instead, he must stay forever to worsen

His new insect body, never alive."
    I looked on this bug and could not
        pity
His new endless being, never to revive.

Circle 9

I walked down the stairs to the final
        round,
    Where Lucifer lived, to punish the
        worst,
His angels of darkness innumerous did
        abound

To see that each sinner received his
        reward.
    I walked on, looking at every face,
Each filled with horror, disdain and
        discord.

Kevorkian's eyes then looked back at
        me,
    Filled with hatred and pain, undying
        remorse.
I knew his great sin, no weeping banshee

Had to inform me of what he had done.
    This was the cell of the killers of
        men,

Who needed no weapon, no skill and no
        gun.

They were entrusted with a patient's life,
    But took advantage of their noble
        rank,
And killed their client, no scratch with a
        knife.

"These tormented souls," the spirit then
        told me,
    "Are known as the Murderous MDs,
Racked with every pain of Allah's
        decree.

Their sentence is eternity of death,
    By burning, by crushing, by torture,
        et al.
Without delight, bereft of living breath.

They continue to die after they're dead
    And the only memory which
        sustains
Is that of the pain of death, feeling
        instead

Of happiness: abhorrence, anguish, woe;
    Forever condemned to death of the
        soul."
    Kevorkian then asked for a quid pro quo,

Bargaining for a chance to change his
life.
The Devil laughed and said, "You
have no life,"
Then beat him with stripes to add to his
strife.

"Once in Hell, you will in no way get
out,
I am your king; you must do as I
wish."
He then looked at me, and smirked
without doubt.

TWELVE

I always planned on graduating. Things don't always go the way we plan. I knew that I wasn't on the path to graduation, but I was going to make that up with online classes and night school. I needed to make up two semesters of World History, two semesters of United States History, Government, Economics, and six semesters of a language. I had my path set out—I would take World History my senior year along with AP Calculus, AP English Literature, Government, Economics, and Orchestra. I wanted to make up my language credits by taking Japanese during my junior year (3 credits) by taking afternoon classes, and I wanted to make up United States History through correspondence classes or night school. It was perfect.

I was missing these classes because I made some unwise decisions during high school. I took Contemporary Issues instead of Health. I didn't take required classes because I had Orchestra both 0-hour and 1st period. I took a church class called Seminary each year, which I believe was not an unwise decision, but it left me one credit short each year. However, I could have made up the credits. I could have graduated. But nursing stopped me.

It was the time commitment. I still had some hope that I could graduate, but it grew slim when I started signing up for my senior year classes. I could not take Calculus because it conflicted with nursing and with Seminary. With nursing every morning, I could have taken English, World History, and United States History, and then finished my day with a little night school for Government and Economics. But where would I ever find time for homework? Better yet, how would I make up six semesters of a language?

I knew I would not graduate when I started my senior year. I signed up for classes that I thought would benefit me the most. With my new senior year schedule, a miracle happened—I got my life back. I found time for friends. I found time to practice my viola. I found time to join wrestling once again. I found time to join a Pre-med club and a Junior Medical Reserve Corps. I found time for fun.

I think I might have started to overdo it with some of my activities. Take, for example, wrestling:

11-25-06

...I continued to go to wrestling. During pre-season, and before warming up and stretching, I wrestled Tom, got him in a wicked head-and-arm, and slammed him into a pin. He got a look of horror on his face and let out a small cry. I guess I badly strained and tore his trapezius, so he was out all of pre-season.

Soon enough, season started, and I was getting really good (not to brag, or anything). I was definitely going varsity, probably 189 because I weighed 180 lbs and kept gaining. I could beat everyone and was having a great time, and Tom came back, which made me happy because he is actually pretty good and fun to wrestle. However, the first time we wrestled live, I shot in to take him down. Right when my right knee hit the ground, I heard a nasty "POP!" I tried to stand up but couldn't because my leg locked up and had some extreme pain. I thought I had dislocated my knee or something, so I went to the trainer. He told me he thought I might have torn my meniscus, or the outer layer of cartilage in my knee.

I was on crutches and went to my doctor, then to an orthopedic specialist. A physician's assistant told me that I just badly strained my lateral collateral ligament (LCL). I was relieved it wasn't a torn meniscus, but I was still sad. It's somewhat ironic since I had injured Tom the previous time we wrestled. He told me that he got his revenge...

12-29-06

...I got an MRI done on my knee today, but I haven't gotten the results. I got a second opinion on my knee a while back, and the doctor believes that I didn't sprain my LCL but that I stretched and damaged my anterior cruciate ligament (ACL). That stupid

physician's assistant, misdiagnosing me. I have probably done more damage since I didn't have the necessary surgery right away...

...I got my MRI done on my knee, but stupid Lacelove makes tons of mistakes and won't admit it. On my MRI, they wrote "Unable to visualize LCL clearly due to patient movement and poor patient positioning." Now, I looked at those images and saw no movement. As for positioning, do you really believe that was my fault?!?!?! Anyway, the results point to a medially torn meniscus, but I won't know until Wednesday, which is my orthopedics appointment with a different doctor (starting the New Year, we finally got away from Lacelove and are now with Universal Healthcare and Presbyterian). We'll see how that goes...

On Thursday, I went to the Ney's house for a little party, but within the first two minutes I was pelted with snowballs and the interior of my car was filled with snow. I got on the girls team of this snowball fight and decided to tackle Naegle. However, as I ran, I misjudged how deep the snow was and took a little fall. I tried to get back up, but my knee gave out—it was super painful! Crap! I hurt my knee even more! So, I whipped out the crutches from the trunk of my car and started using them again. Before, I was to the point where I was jump roping and using the elliptical machine for hours without having knee pain. Then, I couldn't even walk. However, it got to feeling better, so I think it's about back to where it was before...

On February 9, 2007, I experienced the first surgery of my life. I was a bit apprehensive, even though I have seen multiple surgeries being performed. Maybe that added to my apprehension, having observed Cesarean sections, open-heart surgeries (coronary artery bypass grafts—CABG), open brain surgeries (one in which a meningioma on the right frontal lobe was removed), and various orthopedic procedures.

The morning of my surgery, I went to nursing and took notes. I didn't want to miss lecture just because I was having little tools poked into my knee. I wore nice comfy clothes including scrub bottoms and a worn out t-shirt. Arriving at the hospital at 1:00 pm for my pre-op preparations, I already knew what to expect. Or so I thought.

It was the first time in my life that part of my leg was shaved, and I'm hoping it will be the last. My leg was then scrubbed with a cold, yellow betadine solution.

I had my first IV started in my left hand, which was not so pleasant. I am usually not bad with needles, but I have seen so many IVs started in hands that I cringed when I imagined the nurse poking around in *my* hand for the vein. Luckily, it was numbed first, but even when I looked away, I could tell that the nurse was struggling to find a nice blood supply. That is just not a very good image.

It is a lot different being in the role of a patient rather than the nurse. It was actually kind of nice. I was given Versed through my IV, and it helped to make me calm, but it didn't really take away my memories of what happened until right up until I was given general anesthesia. I learned, however, that I love general anesthesia! What a wonderful creation! I went out in just a few seconds, and I woke up after the surgery. Isn't it wonderful?

However, things weren't fine and dandy. As it turns out, the fall that I sustained in the infamous snowball fight must have injured my meniscus and ACL even more. Instead of a simple clipping of the torn cartilage and weight bearing the very next day, a large portion of my meniscus was torn. Luckily, it was on the outer most edge where there is a slight blood supply. There was a chance that my meniscus could be saved! My doctor stitched together the torn meniscus with three sutures. Because my ACL felt loose, he used a neat little heating tool to contract the ligament and make it tight. In order to help my meniscus to heal, he also did a procedure called micro puncturing. He poked tiny holes in my bones and tissue around the meniscus in order to get more blood to the site and facilitate healing.

Following my surgery, I had the worst pain of my life. I was told to not bear any weight on my right leg for six weeks after the surgery. That was no contemplation for me, for when I even tried to stand upright, I could feel blood rushing to my surgery site, a sharp, pounding pain resonating throughout my knee. I took the maximum amount of Vicodin that I was allowed to take in a day before killing my liver. I stayed in bed, yet there was too much to do!

Starting Sunday, I went to church and youth rehearsals for a musical in which I was performing. I then went straight back to school, and though the pain got somewhat manageable, it would not go away. When I saw my doctor for a follow up appointment, he saw that my knee was incredibly swollen. "That is where the pain is coming from," he told me. "You need to take time off to elevate your knee and ice it!" But how could I? School has always been a priority for me!

I knew that my doctor was right, that I needed to take care of myself. I told myself that the next day I would take off from school and not get out of bed unless absolutely necessary. That was where the miracle happened: that evening it snowed. And it snowed. It didn't stop until the afternoon following, meaning that we had a snow day! What convenient timing, eh?

I spent all day with my leg elevated on around ten to fifteen pillows with fresh ice intermittently covering my knee (which was covered with ace-wrap, of course). After that, I continued to elevate and ice my knee whenever possible. It worked so well that immediately I got off Vicodin and started to take ibuprofen instead. I became almost religious in practicing my physical therapy exercises, wanting my knee to recover its strength and range of motion. Already, my quadriceps and calves were considerably atrophied. What a sad sight!

My surgery is part of the reason I decided to drop out of high school. I had to miss some theory time in nursing because of physical therapy and the like, but I also was not allowed to work in the hospital until I was completely off crutches. That means I missed all of pediatric clinicals, which is a real bummer because it was the only rotation I was really looking forward to. In my nursing class, I was required to make up hour for hour. That would have been a very difficult task to accomplish if I had both nursing and high school. What a relief it was to only have nursing homework to work on!

THIRTEEN

2-24-07

...PEDIATRIC clinicals start this week, so I'm gonna have to be making up tons of time (probably 30+ hours). Because of post-op appointments and physical therapy, I also have to make up theory time. I made up five hours this week with helping the nursing assistant class with bed making and with bed baths. Oh my gosh, it was horrible. It took one of the guys over half and hour to make an unoccupied bed. How is that possible?!?! I don't think I was that bad when I was learning... But who knows? I was a crazy junior back in those days. It took my entire time to try to get the three guys done with one unoccupied bed change, one occupied bed change, and one bed bath.

When I was writing my previous journal entry, I was all drugged up on Vicodin. Do you notice if I sound spacey or anything? I have noticed that drugs really mess with my schoolwork. The Monday after my surgery, I took two Vicodin before school and I took three tests. One of those was my newborn test, in which I scored an 83%. Strange since I love babies and know lots about them. The next test in nursing was over infants, before which I only took one Vicodin. I scored a 91%. The next test I took was the toddler test. I took no Vicodin, only a few ibuprofen (600 mg). Everyone was getting in the 70s and low 80s. I got a 98%. Coincidence? I think not! Drugs mess with my brain! So here's the lesson—no narcotics on a test day. Yup.

Oh, I forgot. On the day after my surgery, I did get visitors: Naegle, Baby D, Sara and Megan, and Kirsten (the girls visited separate from the guys). We played Wii. I killed them all while drugged up and sitting down. I gave the Cherry Hills Ward girls a hard time in church (while sitting in my wheel chair) that three Bear Canyon Ward girls visited me and they didn't. How lame. But it was cool. The Sorensens also visited and brought me junk food and movies, and Brother Hermele brought me a shower chair (a lifesaver until I got my skin sutures out, just last Tuesday).

Okay, let's see... School is pretty tough with surgery, and I'm getting real bad senioritis where I don't want to do anything. So, I'm dropping out of high school this Wednesday. Crazy, eh? I'm gonna be a high school dropout! Here's the reason: I need my GED by nursing graduation in May, and I need to make up a crud load of hours because of my surgery. Moreover, I need to have proof that I am not enrolled in public schools in order to take my GED. The real reason for dropping out: senioritis. So, I get my entire afternoon off starting this Wednesday, February 28th. Fun, eh? That'll be such a relief. I'm still planning to take the AP exams, so I guess I'll study on my own...

As this journal entry verifies, I didn't hesitate to drop out. In fact, I *wanted* to get out of high school as soon as possible. I was sick of doing mindless work and not really getting anything out of it. When I told my parents that I wanted to drop out of high school, and that I had made an appointment with my counselor the following week to do so, my parents had some interesting things to say:

"Go right ahead," my dad told me. "Maybe with your extra time we can do more backpacking as a family!"

"Sure," said my mom, "as long as you go out to eat with me and to more movies during the day."

I had approval. Most parents wouldn't be so enthusiastic about their kid telling them that they are sick of high school and want to dropout. My parents actually encouraged me to do so. I will tell you, though, that I have fulfilled my mom's wish to a greater extent than I thought possible. And believe me, once my knee recovers I am definitely continuing with some awesome backpacking trips with my dad.

I had to ask myself, however, why my parents would be so encouraging. In fact, my mom seems to tell everyone proudly that her son is a high school dropout, even the cashiers at the grocery store. I've gotten mixed emotions from people who hear this. "Why?" seems to be the common question with adults. "Lucky!" seems to be a common response among people my age. To the adults I explain, and to the teens, I rub it in that they still have to go to school. However, even though I technically dropped out, I really don't see it that way. It is not the end, but the beginning of a new life.

In November of 2006, I applied for the only two universities that I was sincerely considering: Brigham Young University and the University of New Mexico. At first, I thought of the fact that I didn't want to stay in state for school. I had the notion that UNM was a poor school and that I would not get the best education that I could. BYU was the place for me. I could be social and still learn. I could have fun and maybe even meet my future wife.

The reason I applied to UNM was because they actually have a medical school, unlike BYU, and there is a program called the BA/MD program in which I could be accepted to medical school as a senior in high school. I guess you could say that I was just curious of how I would do.

For BYU, I was accepted with no problem. I talked to the director of admissions, and based on my six semester GPA (3.93 due to A minuses… grrrr…) and ACT score (32/36), I would have a two-semester full tuition scholarship (renewable for all four years). That didn't sound too bad, but I was disappointed because in order to be considered for an eight-semester full tuition scholarship, I needed an ACT score of 33. However, the director of admissions also gave me a free t-shirt, so I was sure that I was going to BYU.

When I applied for UNM's BA/MD program, I didn't realize that I would also be considered for the Regents' Scholarship. In fact, I didn't even know what the Regents' Scholarship was. I received a letter in the mail saying that I was a semi-finalist and giving me an interview time to be considered a finalist. This was exciting because I had never before been offered any type of scholarship with a name to it. I looked it up online, and lo and behold, it just so happened that the Regents' was UNM's top scholarship.

Needless to say, I took the interview seriously, but I still wasn't sure of where I would actually go to school. There were two interviews, each with a small group of administrators, scholarship committee members, and present Regents' scholars. The first group I interviewed with was relaxed and fun. I did well and tried to let my personality show. The second group, however, was stern and serious, asking difficult questions.

In the first group, I was asked questions such as, "If you could have lunch with any one person from the past, who would it be and why?" It was more of a conversation than an interview, making it much easier to be myself.

In the second group, I was asked questions such as, "If you were governor of New Mexico, what would you do in order to help cultural ties and assimilation?" and, "If you were a physician hired by an interrogation team that was interrogating a criminal for information, and you were responsible for telling the team how far they could go, how far would you let them go?"

During each of the interviews, I kept my calm and came up with a thoughtful answer, trying to let my personality come out. I guess it helped that I have been through interviews before, and I also have been an interviewer with patients in gaining history. After the interviews were over, I should have heard the results in just a few days. After a week passed, I heard some of my friends had been rejected, including some of my nursing classmates and many of the valedictorians at my high school. Being rejected still isn't too bad because they still got the Presidential scholarship, which pays for full tuition for eight semesters.

After three weeks passed, I finally got a letter in the mail. I was selected to be a Regents' Scholarship recipient! I immediately perused the acceptance letter and found that this offer was too good to give up—full tuition, books, room and board, etc. I would pay nothing for school; in fact, if I spent less than they gave me, I would be paid to go to school. Moreover, UNM's medical school is one of the top in the country. This wasn't sounding like such a bad school after all. I would be getting a private mentor based on my major and have the opportunity to study abroad by only paying travel fees. Let me tell you this—work does pay off.

FOURTEEN

*I*T'S *official—I'm a high school dropout as of February 28th. Fun. On Monday, I went to school as usual, finding that it was pretty useless. So, on Tuesday I ditched all day (with nursing clinicals, I get the entire day off because of my knee). Wednesday was the dropout day, and now my life has become a heck of a lot less stressful. Now I actually have time for myself.*

Another added bonus, yet detriment in the future—without being able to do clinicals, I get Monday through Wednesday almost completely off, though I'm still attending Seminary every day. Sure, I'm going to have to make up my clinical hours eventually, but not yet! With all my extra time, I get to practice my viola, read good books (I just finished <u>Freakonomics</u>), work on my knee and other muscles, and occasionally play some Nintendo Wii. I just wish that I could walk, but I still have to wait until the 21st, two weeks from this Wednesday.

I've decided that after I get better, I'm going to get in amazing shape and get a nice tan for my lady fans. Yup, that sounds like a worthwhile way to spend my time. I love my life. My knee is still progressing faster than anyone anticipated, but I'm not allowed to bear weight none-the-less. I guess I'm kind of cheating on that end with some touch-down weight bearing, but life would be near impossible without that. Well, that's my life. See ya.

I guess you can say that I'm a failure. I do what I want to do. If I want to play some Nintendo, I'll do it. If I want to eat something fatty and delicious, I'll do it. If I want to drop out of high school, I'll do it. However, I know that in everything we do, there are consequences. Playing too many games will turn my brain to mush. Eating too many doughnuts will clog my arteries. It's all about moderation in every aspect of our lives.

I quite karate not knowing this simple truth of consequences. I joined wrestling realizing that I wanted to change my lazy habits so that I could feel good about myself. I quit wrestling because I felt that I was in good shape physically, but not mentally, so I focused more on academics. I did realize, however, that I was backtracking without physical activity, so during my senior year I started wrestling again. I quit, this time because of an injury. However, once I recover from surgery, I am planning to be more physically active and progressing to where I once was.

I quit choir in 8th grade, knowing that I'm not the best singer and that orchestra was more for me. However, I still sing and enjoy doing so. I participate in barbershop quartets. I am also singing solos in an upcoming church production called From Cumorah's Hill, a presentation on the Book of Mormon.

I also dropped out of orchestra, again wanting to continue my education. Earlier I said that I still play for myself, and this is true. But, I play for others as well. I am currently playing in From Cumorah's Hill orchestra, which accompanies the choir. I continue to practice and am planning to join orchestra once enrolled college.

When I dropped out of high school, I was not looking for a nice break, though that did accompany this action. I was looking out for my needs and my future. I needed to make up many hours for nursing. I also did not have the classes necessary for graduation. High school is for the preparation for college, and I feel that I prepared well. What else do I need? I am not going to stop my education; in fact, I will probably be in college for longer than I was enrolled in public schools.

Life often contains the unexpected. I think that fear of the unknown drives us to be timid and insecure. Just the other day in nursing, one of my fellow students, a girl named Tuesdaye, put a quote by President Robert F. Kennedy on the board: "Only those who dare to fail greatly can ever achieve greatly." Put away fear, and dare to fail greatly. It is only by seeking to do something great that we can ever move forward in life.

I always ask myself, "What is the worst that could happen?" When performing in front of a large audience (something that most people aren't too comfortable with), I ask myself this same question. The worst-case scenario for me would go something like this:

I get up to sing, not feeling too bad. I walk onto the stage and get up to the microphone, my armpits starting to sweat. As the accompaniment starts to play, my hands start shaking, progressively moving down to my knees. It's not too bad as the music starts; the people all seem so far away. But all eyes are focused on me. Immediately before my entrance, I start feeling light-headed and weak. I don't faint, but that is not necessarily a good thing. I would have rather passed out.

I start my solo, the only accompaniment a piano and soft woodwind instruments in the background. My voice starts to croak, and I cannot seem to hit any of the notes. It's as if I was going through puberty all over again: my voice squeaks up and down, a sound similar to a dying cat. I'm too close to the microphone, my piercing squeals making audience members flinch. I feel my face flush, and the sweating comes more profusely. Everyone in the choir and orchestra behind me sees my dress shirt covered with sweat stains, as does the first few rows of the audience.

I see members of the audience trying to keep a straight face, but I can tell that they are being entertained. There are children who, unable to hide their true emotions, say in a loud voice, "Mommy! Why is he squeaking?" I hear members of the choir behind me, holding back their chuckles. Tears of embarrassment start streaming down my face as I quickly run (or hobble, as I am still on crutches) off the stage and into the bathroom, for the first time realizing that I not only sounded dreadful, but I looked like a retched mess.

Is that it? Well, that wasn't too bad, now was it? Yes, if this actually happened, I would be embarrassed and would try to hide until everyone had left. However, is this really so bad? Let's look at it one piece at a time.

At a performance like the one I would be singing at, most of the people in the audience are people you don't know. They will feel bad for you, they will want to help you but know they cannot. Yet, though they may remember the experience of the incredible squeaking boy and may ridicule you in private, they will not remember your face in a month or two, especially if they were sitting further back.

As for the members of the choir who actually know you, you must have been singing better than they had if you have the solo. It was just one episode of stage fright. Most likely, the members of the choir and orchestra can put themselves in your shoes and realize how you must feel—you worked hard, and at the moment you had been anticipating for several months, your dreams are smashed. They can help console you and comfort you during this hard time.

After the immediate is over, what next? You will most likely not die from this experience. Your future isn't ruined (unless, perhaps, you are a professional performer). You will still have your friends and family to support you (and if you don't, you might want to try to find new friends). In a year, you will look back at this experience and laugh. But more than that, you will grow from this situation. You might feel more comfortable speaking or performing publicly, having been through the worst and realizing that it didn't do anything to your spirits in the long run. You know that you can handle intense ridicule and embarrassment, so you no longer have that fear stopping your progression in the world. In addition, you will know that singing in front of large groups of people just isn't your thing.

So why not dare to fail greatly? As demonstrated in the situation before, even when we fail we can learn and grow from the experience. Moreover, if we do well, we are so much the better for it. How can we ever prove to ourselves that we *can* do well if we don't *try* to do well in something great? If we fail, we'll fail with grandeur, with the knowledge that we tried something great and did the best we can. The knowledge gleaned from trying is invaluable.

Now take Senior Prom, for instance. Would you be willing to go if you were on crutches? What if you weren't even a high school student?

This was the question recently going through my head. I never really thought about it before, mainly because I didn't even know Prom was coming up. But, the topic came up at one of our From Cumorah's Hill rehearsals. I started thinking about it and realized that it might actually be fun. In fact, it might be amazing. I mean, what's the worst that could happen?

The girl I wanted to ask, Kirsten, was in the From Cumorah's Hill orchestra with me, in the first violin section. I sat at my computer one night, trying to figure out a way to ask her, but it seemed as though I had a brain block. I started thinking about what might happen—I was probably going against a lot of rules since I wasn't really in high school—and this is a newspaper article I wrote to ask Kirsten:

Crippled High School Dropout Wants To Go To Prom

Boy Did Not Know How To Ask Girl

BY LUCKY THE LEPRECHAUN
Journal Staff Writer

Forced to drop out of high school following a severe case of senioritis, 17-year old Sam Hobbs' dream of attending his last high school dance, La Cueva's Prom on March 17th, was crushed.

Or was it? While sifting through his wallet looking for his mini *For the Strength of Youth* pamphlet, Sam caught a glimpse of a navy blue and silver piece of plastic—his senior ID card.

But would it work? Sam could only hope he wouldn't be spotted by the counselor who withdrew him from school.

Sam quickly crutched through the halls of his former high school, frequently glancing over his shoulder, imagining a school nark tackling him and throwing him off his crutches.

Twice Sam almost fell, scurrying freshmen crowding the main concourse. He bumped hard into a football player, splashing the jock's bitter-smelling caffeinated beverage onto Sam's newly cleaned and ironed BYU t-shirt.

Sam made it into the ticket line and purchased two tickets to Prom. He was set for "An Evening on the Emerald Isle."

Or was he? Sam soon realized that he was crippled and would have an incredibly difficult time finding a girl kind enough to settle for him. He sadly wallowed away in his melancholic state.

The girl he desperately wanted to go with was from another high school, and she probably had better things to do with her time than to entertain a cripple. Was it worth the risk?

As Sam sat in the From Cummorah's Hill orchestra, he glanced at the girl playing her violin, and he couldn't help but think of how lucky he would be and what a wonderful evening he would have with her—if only she would say "Yes!"

Finally, Sam mustered up the courage to ask but could not think of a way that would suit this superlative young woman.

Sam threw up his arms in frustration as he decided to just do it:

Kirsten, will you go to Prom with me?

I taped this article into a newspaper with a picture of me looking desperate on my crutches, holding a bouquet of flowers in my hand. I knew that Kirsten had an early morning class—Seminary—so I stopped by this class, which I do occasionally anyways. I had the Seminary teacher read the article at the beginning of class as if it was part of his lesson. At the end, I asked Kirsten to the dance.

At an orchestra rehearsal following this, Kirsten came up to me after a short break and gave me a chocolate cake. Just a side note—it was incredibly delicious, and I'm pretty sure I gained three pounds the same night. There was a tag on the cake addressed to me, which said, "Saying yes is a piece of cake!" Written on the cake in green letters was the word "yes." (The theme of the dance is "An Evening on the Emerald Isle" because it is taking place on St. Patrick's Day). I was in, and there was no turning back.

What is the worst that can happen now? Well, I have the tickets, and I have a date. If I were kicked out of the dance since I'm not a high school student, I would just go somewhere else with my date and wing it. We could probably have just as good of a time. Plus, it would be quite an adventure. If my date was to stand me up, I could stay home, have more time, and just be out $30 for the tickets. Although both of these scenarios would be disappointing, I think that I could survive without any long-term consequences. But what might happen if I go to the dance as planned? Here is a worst-case scenario:

Before the dance, I want to look the best I possibly can. I ask my mom for a hair cut because the sides are getting a little too bushy and I'm looking like a "box-head," and she happily agrees. She starts by using electric hair clippers to shorten the sides and back of my head. As she runs the device through my hair, the guard suddenly falls off, as it wasn't properly locked into place, drawing a shaven line across the side of my head.

Of course, I get upset—it is only a few hours before the dance, and I really don't look good with a buzz cut. But, there is nothing I can do now. My head is shaven, and I get ready for the dance. Trying to make my new shaven head seem less bald, I forget about putting on deodorant. I hurry into my room and throw on my suit.

Because I am still worrying about how I look, I forget to pick up the corsage and mother's flower that I ordered (and paid for, nonetheless). Moreover, my parents have to drive me since I still can't walk. I hurry and hobble up to the front door, giving a nice solid knock. Without even speaking with her parents or complimenting her on her dress, I usher Kirsten hurriedly to the car.

Trying to be a gentleman, I open the door for Kirsten. I close it too soon, however, getting her dress and her finger caught in the door. She lets out a yelp as I mutter an apology and hop to the opposite side of the car, my parents smiling back at us from the front. "How can this possibly get worse?" I think to myself. If only I knew.

My parents drop us off at the restaurant for dinner and decide that they might as well stay and eat there as well. Then, adding to that idea, they decide to join us. I am uncomfortable as my parents sit adjacent to me and my date. "You two look *so* cute together," my mom says, her chin wresting on the backs of her hands while she gazes into our faces. "Let me take a picture. You two need to get married!" I can tell that Kirsten is feeling a bit out of place, as am I, due to my mother's flight of thoughts that she can't seem to keep to herself.

After an awkward half-hour while waiting for our food, it finally arrives. I make the mistake of ordering pasta, and by the end of dinner, my new shirt and tie are covered in a dense tomato sauce. Unbeknownst to me, I have green fragments of some sort of tomato sauce constituent stuck in my teeth, which stay there all night.

After dinner, my parents drive me and Kirsten to the dance. I am relieved that they will no longer be tagging around. We enter the dance, and I feel a rush of fright as I recognize staff administrators who have the power to kick me out. Luckily, they do not, but there was worse to come.

Kirsten and I feel out of place as there is "dirty dancing" going on all around us. We try to stay in our own little group and ignore the disgusting innuendos of the bumping and grinding of our fellow classmates, yet it is hard to overlook. There is rap music blaring across the dance floor, every other word containing four letters and suggesting the limited vocabulary of the vocalist.

I decide to start having some fun, so I ask Kirsten for a clean dance, and we get off to the side to get away from the crowd. As we start to dance, I start enjoying the evening. However, my fun is short lived as I start to sweat and stink of body odor. My hands start sweating as they do so often. A fellow wrestler then "accidentally" kicks one of the crutches out from under me. My injured leg hits the ground and I fall to the floor, sharp pain shooting from my knee.

I try to stand up, but my knee locks up, and I know that my meniscus is torn again. Since I don't have a ride waiting, Kirsten goes out in search of someone who can take me to the emergency room, but no one is willing to do it. Who would want to leave the dance to go to the hospital? So, we call my parents, and in half an hour, they arrive at the dance.

The rest of the evening for me is spent under anesthesia. As I wake up from the emergency surgery, Kirsten is gone and my parents are frowning above my head. "I had a bad feeling about this dance," my dad whispers to my mom. "At least Kirsten could go home instead of spending her entire night catering to a cripple."

"Kirsten must have had such a horrible evening!" I think to myself. As my head stops spinning and the anesthesia wears off, I get out of bed and wheel chaired out to my parents' car. I go home depressed, embarrassed, and even further disabled. I fall asleep with tears of pity and sorrow for myself (and for my date) caking my eyelashes.

Is that the worst it gets? Again I have to ask, is that really so bad? At the time, it probably looks dire, and indeed, my date probably did not have the best of times. However, this hypothetical situation really isn't very bad.

Let's start with the haircut. I think that this is a fear of many guys who are about to go on a nice date. They want a haircut, but they are afraid of what mistakes the hairdresser might make. But that really isn't so bad for a guy. If you mess up your hair, you can just buzz all of it off. It may not look the best, but it certainly doesn't look that bad, especially in the eyes of another. In fact, this indeed happened during Prom, not to me, but to one of my friends. This young man, John, got his haircut a few hours before prom. After he didn't like the job that was done, so he had his mom shave his entire head. At first, he didn't like it, but after the many compliments he got at the dance, John told me that he was thinking about keeping his head shaved. "Think about the money I could save on shampoo!" he told me.

I have always had a fear of slamming my date's dress or hand in a door. How awful would that be? However, you have to think of what the date is going through. She might have a bruised finger and a crinkled dress. I think that the act of opening the door for her shows her that you respect her and want to be the best you can. So, even if you aren't a "perfect gentleman," if you try, it shows that you care.

Most of the things that can go wrong are little things like spilling food on your clothes or smelling bad. It's embarrassing at the moment, but you can still have fun even if you have a slight case of B.O. Just be yourself, don't beat yourself up over a little tomato sauce stain, and you can probably turn something potentially embarrassing into a fun and lasting memory.

The worst thing that could happen with going to Prom would have to be injuring my knee again, a potential problem. But, I know that my knee is progressing, and in a week, I'd be walking without crutches anyway. And if I did happen to injure my knee and have a second surgery, it would not be as bad as it might sound.

Since I had my meniscus repaired, I am forced to be on crutches for six weeks to let it heal. However, there is still the possibility that it will not heal, meaning that I might need a second surgery anyways. The second surgery would not be a repair; it would be a removal. I wouldn't have to pay anything since I already met my insurance company's deductible after the first surgery. Though I would like to keep every part of my knee, a removal wouldn't be so bad. I could start walking the day after the surgery, so I would lose the crutches a week early. I could still do the activities I enjoy, but I would probably have to substitute swimming for things like running or wrestling. I could still do those activities; I would just run the risk of wearing down the cartilage in my knee and getting arthritis early in life.

What can this worst-case scenario teach me? Well, I guess I'll try not to land on my bad knee if I fall. But if I do, I still have my life in front of me. I can be a better gentleman but know that I don't have to beat myself up over little mistakes. You know, it's a great thing to be prepared for the worst. It relieves the burden of feeling embarrassed when making blundering errors. Everything can work out in the end.

FIFTEEN

3/19/07

WELL, to tell you the truth, I'm feeling like quite a bum without anything to do. Don't get me wrong—I love having time to do things for myself. It's just that it gets a little dull going out to movies with your mom every day and not seeing your friends. Oh well, what can you do? In addition, I hate being unproductive, so I find that I really don't like to watch movies any more. Sure, it's relaxing and enjoyable, but when it's all over, I feel like I wasted my day away. If I devoted two hours of my time every day to something productive instead of watching movies, I could change the world! I could become amazing at the viola! I could become a better man, more prepared to be the best husband and father! Hmm... Maybe I should do that...

Last week my mom asked me what I was going to do with all my free time. I jokingly said, "I'm going to write a book." My mom asked me, "What are you going to call it?" She was serious, even though I was joking. I thought about it and responded, "Memoirs of a High School Dropout." My mom told me it sounded interesting and wished me luck. So, I went off. Not knowing what to do with my time, I started writing. And I kept writing. I found that I enjoyed pulling my memories and thoughts together. Now, the book is about 100 pages long, and I'm trying to think of a good ending. Since it is a memoir, I don't want my writing to go much past my life right now—I've never been a fan of autobiographies. I just want a snapshot of my life up until now, a picture of my values and thoughts, something for me and my future family to look back on and enjoy.

Let's see... My life is pretty much the same as usual—lots of time for things I want to do. We have been having many practices for From Cumorah's Hill since we had our two performances this past weekend. I think it went pretty well. Plus, Prom was this weekend. It was crazy fun! Here's how everything went down:

On Friday, we had our first __From Cumorah's Hill__ performance. I was extremely nervous for a few reasons. We had tech rehearsals and a dress rehearsal just before the performance (the same week), and to put it simply, we sounded like a classroom of first graders tying to sing "Twinkle-Twinkle Little Star" in unison. Yup, the orchestra was off, the choir was off, the sound and lighting was off, and the soloists, including myself, were off. Could we ever pull it together in one week?

During our dress rehearsal Thursday evening, the director decided to run the practice twice through. It took us about two hours to get through the first time, probably because we had to stop every five minutes or so. But, the second time we went through, we actually sounded quite good. I was amazed. It was a miracle that we did so well. There were some mistakes, such as with the spot light and certain songs with intonation, but they were ever so slight. The orchestra needed quite a bit of work, but I may just be critical because of some of the other groups I have performed with.

When I sang my solo, I was only nervous the moment I got on stage. My one knee started shaking a little (the one supporting me, since I'm still not allowed to bear weight on my left knee), but it wasn't too bad. I stood a good distance from the microphone, and I did surprisingly well. That made me so happy! I messed up a little on the ends of phrases, and I said "they" instead of "we" at one part, but no one seemed to notice—not even the ones who tutored and coached me for this song. Cool.

I was also nervous because of the number of people who came to watch—it was probably around 500-600 people, including a few of my friends I invited. Afterwards, I got a lot of compliments, which really boosted my confidence and self-esteem. You know, I am not a performer. In fact, I almost hate *performing by myself because I am not one to feel comfortable in front of people. I think I'm talented, but it is hard to share those talents because I'm shy. I'm working at it, though. It was totally worth it. Do you think my singing gained me some more lady fans? I hope so... Just kidding.*

Saturday was Prom. Yes, I actually went. Here's my story: I wasn't planning on going. I mean, I'm on crutches, what was I supposed to do at a dance? Hop around? But, two Sundays ago, after the __From Cumorah's Hill__ rehearsal, Sara came up to me and told me I should go with her group to La Cueva's Prom and that I should take Kirsten. At first, I pointed at my crutches and gave her a look that said, "What would be the point of me going to a dance?" But, I started thinking about it, and I realized that I can do a lot on crutches. Plus, if I could go with Kirsten, I could have an amazing time!

If you don't remember, the first date I went on where I actually asked the girl was with Kirsten. I realized that I wasn't a very good gentleman on that date—I mean, she drove to my house, and I didn't even walk her to her car! That was going to change. But, how could I ask her? And how would she respond? I wanted to do something with the dance theme ("An Evening on the Emerald Isle"—the dance was on St. Patrick's Day), but that is a very difficult theme to work with. So, I sat at the computer, clueless of what to do.

I happened to come across the newspaper article when I was punched in the face in eighth grade (I had it pulled out for my book), so I decided that it would be kind of funny to write an article. I wrote up a funny little article describing the process in which I obtained the tickets—especially since I'm not a high school student. It also went through how I could not find a way to ask the perfect girl. The article was titled: "Crippled High School Dropout Wants to go to Prom." I thought that was pretty funny. I had brother Rogers read the article during early morning seminary while I came and visited. At the very end, I asked Kirsten out.

Following this incident, at a <u>From Cumorah's Hill</u> practice, Kirsten answered by giving me an amazing chocolate cake with the word "Yes" written with green icing. On a tag it said, "Sam, saying yes is a piece of cake!" How cool is that? So, I was in, and we went to Prom. We went in a group of 12, consisting of Spencer and Claire, Cameron and Christa, Jacob and Sara, Justin and Taylor (who moved here from Japan a little while ago), Brad and a freshman girl from choir, and me and Kirsten. I had a blast, and I hope Kirsten did as well. I think it was the most fun date and group I've gone with.

I found that Kirsten is a lot like me, though probably a lot better. She likes chemistry and biology (especially DNA and viruses, etc). She wants to go to medical school and study virology, which is pretty cool. Unlike me, she is an incredible athlete. Plus, she can eat! For dinner, we went to Azuma's Teppan Grill. At first, we told our dates we were going to Sonic, and many of them believed us, especially when we pulled into the Sonic parking lot. However, Azuma's was right across the street and we had reservations.

Before, we were going to go to an Italian restaurant in the Albuquerque Uptown plaza, but because Kirsten and I joined, we couldn't change the reservations from 10 to 12 people. Oh well, I think Azuma's was better. We had sushi, steaks, etc. It was incredible. I've had too many dates where the girl eats like nothing and is unwilling to try something new. Kirsten had never eaten sushi, but after I showed her how, she went at it! I made a really mild wasabi mixture at first for dipping, but with each piece of sushi, I increased the wasabi concentration. By the end, we were practically dipping the sushi into pure wasabi, being as liberal as if it was guacamole. It was amazingly fun, even though we both started to cry from the burning.

The sushi we had weren't just the rolls—it was nigiri (raw fish slices on top of a small amount of rice). We had maguro (tuna), unagi (eel), etc. Yum. Yup, I have to say that Kirsten is an amazing date. I told her that we have to go out for sushi again sometime. I'm planning to ask her over spring break and go on a double with Justin. That should be crazy awesome.

Azuma's was a fun but expensive restaurant. Our cook had fun with Spencer, throwing green beans into his moth with the spatula, etc. The cook was pretty amazing, and it was fun to watch. There was lots of fire and tricks with cooking the food. Plus, the cuisine was excellent. We had meat, fried rice, miso soup, salad, tempura, sushi, etc. The total (just for me and Kirsten) ended up being about $70—$50 for dinner and $20 for sushi. It was so worth it! Justin ended up paying $80 for dinner, and he helped me finish off what I ordered (he can eat a ton, to say the least). I'm just grateful because my parents helped me out with the tickets and corsage. I would be so broke if I had to pay for everything! It's a good thing I didn't rent a tuxedo—I just wore a suit with a blue shirt and dark blue patterned tie. It was pretty nice. At dinner, I demonstrated how to eat with chopsticks and how little kids eat who haven't learned to use them yet, and in the process, I spilled grease and soy sauce on my clothes. Oh well, it was only a few dark spots.

Following dinner, we headed off to the dance. We took two vehicles to the dance—Spencer's Denali and the Justin's "Mormon Wagon," both of which were super nice on the inside. We made it to the convention center fashionably late, which is nice because we didn't have to wait in any lines to get in. No one questioned me about being a high school dropout, so I was good to go. I had a lot of fun. We boogied all night! Kirsten and I made up a one-legged salsa, slow dance, etc. It was crazy fun, and I still think I can dance better than most of those "dirty dancers" there. I have never been to Prom before, and I found it to be kind of nice because there were less people there and I knew almost everyone.

Let's see, Andrea was announced as Prom Queen, so that was pretty cool. Plus, this was the first dance in which there were a few songs that weren't rap. Yay! However, the music was still loud, so I had to yell to talk to Kirsten. Following the dance, we went to the Steel's house for breakfast at midnight. We had crepes, and even though I was full from dinner, I kept eating, and so did Kirsten. Man, she's perfect! Yeah, it was awesome. We hung around at the Steel's house talking and enjoying ourselves, and I took Kirsten home a little after one. I got to bed a little after two. I had to get up for church early, but it was still worth it.

I wanted to take a nap after church, but I ended up having tons of meeting to go to—Bishop's Youth Council, Aaronic Priesthood Committee Meeting, two youth visits, two home teaching appointments, etc. I had about an hour to do some physical therapy exercises for my leg before having to head off for our last <u>From Cumorah's Hill</u> performance. I forgot to take my allergy medication (it is one of the worst allergy seasons ever!), I got a bloody nose during one of my home teaching visits that left blood coagulated within my throat, and I had lost my voice during Prom. No wonder I didn't do too great on my solo. To top it off, I didn't warm up before I sang. What was I thinking?

To tell you the truth, Sunday's performance was much worse than Friday's. It was awful. People forgot their lines (including one of the best soloists), the microphones weren't working, and everyone just seemed off. Maybe it was due to the one day off on Saturday. I don't know. But, it was sad because there were even more

people there than on Friday. Every seat was filled in the cultural hall, and there were
people standing in the back. I'm guessing we had around 800-900 people there.

I don't know what happened during my solo. Sure, I had everything going
wrong with my voice this day, but everything started all right. I was just as nervous as
last time. When I got to the second phrase of the song, my voice croaked. It cracked up
and down pretty badly, but I quickly got back to the correct note. However, on the next
phase I croaked again. I have never done that before, so I was disappointed that it
happened this time with a larger audience than before. But, I finished out fairly strong,
and I didn't do too badly. It was just a couple of really bad notes, that's all. It's not the
end of my life.

Following the performance, I still got a lot of compliments, but hardly anyone
brought up the fact that my voice cracked, even when I brought it up. Maybe they
thought that the more compliments I was given, the more likely I was to forget the bad
parts of the song. But, I am still glad that people thought I did all right, and I am
content with my performance. It was a good learning experience, nonetheless.

Following the production, the youth involved in the musical gathered in the
chapel for a short slide show presentation and testimony meeting where we could
share our thoughts on the production. It went over an hour overtime, which was
somewhat annoying. At first people got up hesitantly to speak, yet in the middle it
seemed that everyone got up at the same time to sit in the stands and talk over the
pulpit. It was as though there were more people waiting to talk than were listening. It
was still cool, even though I got sick of hearing, "I really didn't want to do this, but it
was awesome in the end."

Oh well, the production of From Cumorah's Hill *is over now and I am back to*
my life as a high school dropout. It's still nice, but I really want to be more productive.
That's why I can't wait to get off crutches in the next couple of weeks—I can finally
start running and get my leanness, muscle tone, and tan back! Just kidding. I guess that
is part of the reason I started writing a book—I want to be productive. My parents
think I should get it published when I am done, but I'm really not that great of a writer.
I guess I'll need a lot of editing if I'm going to do something like that…

EPILOGUE

I sat at the computer, struggling for the end of my book just like I struggled to ask Kirsten to Prom. How can I possibly end a book on my life when my life is nowhere near finished? So, I asked my parents for suggestions. That wasn't too helpful.

Both my mom and my dad first suggested ending it "with a bang." Not only was that not helpful, it probably wasn't the best choice of words. I really don't want to end the book of my life "with a bang," especially since bangs usually come from guns.

"Who is your nemesis?" asked my dad. "You need a nemesis. It could be Naegle. You can call him Volde-Naegle!" Again, not too helpful. Plus, that would probably be some infringement of copyright laws, although I do enjoy reading *Harry Potter*. I'm trying to keep this book as factual as possible, and I am sure that I've never called Naegle "Volde-Naegle" before.

My mom then made the suggestion of keeping it open so that I could write another volume if I so choose. Do I really want to write more about my life? Better yet, would anyone want to read about me for more than one hundred pages? However, I realize now that it is somewhat hard not to keep the end of this book open, for my life will continue after this day (knock on wood).

Who really knows what the future holds in store? In 20 years, I may find myself as a beauty school dropout. However, I know that I have potential, as do millions out there who don't apply themselves as they could. They settle for less than what they are worth. They are afraid of what might happen.

I guess my advice to anyone who cares to listen would be this: dare to be more than you are. Set aside fear, and ask yourself, "What's the worst that can happen?" Better yet, "What's the best that can happen?" Think about the benefits of going and trying something new, being more than a common Joe (no offense to anyone named Joe out there).

The difference between an ordinary person and one who is successful lies in what they do with their lives and individual circumstances. The successful person is wise and applies knowledge for his or her benefit. The person who lives an ordinary lifestyle may have the necessary knowledge but not be able to derive a conclusion.

In middle school, I was once asked, "What is the difference between knowledge and wisdom?" Many dictionaries will tell you that wisdom is the application of knowledge, or it is having knowledge and enlightenment. When this question was asked of me, I sat and thought.

And I thought.

Finally, I came up with an answer that I thought was accurate. What is the difference between knowledge and wisdom? I answered that knowledge is learning from the mistakes that *you* make. Wisdom is learning from the mistakes that *others* make. It's as simple as that.

www.ingramcontent.com/pod-product-compliance
Lightning Source LLC
Chambersburg PA
CBHW020915090426
42736CB00008B/650